SCHOENBERG'S SERIAL ODYSSEY

SCHOENBERG'S SERIAL ODYSSEY

The Evolution of his Twelve-tone Method,
1914–1928

ETHAN HAIMO

CLARENDON PRESS · OXFORD
1990

Oxford University Press, Walton Street, Oxford OX2 6DP

Oxford New York Toronto
Delhi Bombay Calcutta Madras Karachi
Petaling Jaya Singapore Hong Kong Tokyo
Nairobi Dar es Salaam Cape Town
Melbourne Auckland

and associated companies in
Berlin Ibadan

Oxford is a trade mark of Oxford University Press

Published in the United States
by Oxford University Press, New York

British Library Cataloguing in Publication Data
Haimo, Ethan
Schoenberg's serial odyssey: the
evolution of his twelve-tone method.
1. Austrian music. Schoenberg, Arnold,
1874–1951. Critical studies
I. Title   780′.92′4
ISBN 0–19–315260–6

Library of Congress Cataloging in Publication Data
Haimo, Ethan, 1950–
Schoenberg's serial odyssey: the evolution of his twelve-tone
method / Ethan Haimo.
Bibliography: p.   Includes index.
1. Schoenberg, Arnold, 1874–1951—Criticism and interpretation.
2. Twelve-tone system. I. Title.
ML410.S283H33   1989
781.3—dc19   88-19617
ISBN 0–19–315260–6

Typeset by Eta Services (Typesetters) Ltd., Beccles, Suffolk

Printed in Great Britain by
St Edmundsbury Press Ltd., Bury St Edmunds, Suffolk

to the memory of my father,
FRANKLIN TEPPER HAIMO

Preface

MORE than sixty years have passed since Arnold Schoenberg revealed to the world his new method of 'composition with twelve tones related only to one another'. From his remarks to his students and others, it is clear that he believed that the twelve-tone method would have great historical importance. But even Schoenberg, accustomed as he was to both fame and controversy, could not possibly have anticipated all of the many consequences of his discovery.

Perhaps he should have expected that in short order his critics—and there were many—would seize upon his disclosure and use it as the means to vilify both him and his music. Surely it should have come as no surprise that terms such as 'mathematician', 'constructor', and 'unmusical' would be employed by those critics with the certain knowledge that such expressions would be received sympathetically by a conservative musical public, eager to validate its dislike both of atonality and those who practised it.

Perhaps it was also predictable that his new method would be received so enthusiastically by that small group of students and admirers that constituted his circle. Certainly it should have come as no surprise that his former students Alban Berg and Anton von Webern—among others—would adopt the new method in their own compositions. Nor should it have seemed strange that from this circle would emanate sharply worded defences of Schoenberg and his new idea. Of course, it was from this group of supporters that the claim was made that the twelve-tone system should be seen as the inevitable culmination of the sweep of musical history, the logical, perhaps the *only* logical consequence of the evolution of dissonance treatment through the ages.

However, some of the other consequences of Schoenberg's revolution could not possibly have been foreseen. Could Schoenberg have imagined that within a few years his twelve-tone method would be castigated both by the Communists in Russia as anti-proletarian, and by the Nazis in Germany as international (i.e. Jewish)? Or, could he have predicted that after the Second World War the twelve-tone method he had discovered would suddenly become the rallying point for a surprisingly vigorous avant-garde in Europe? Could anyone have guessed that some of the members of the post-war avant-garde would reject Schoenberg's twelve-tone music as impossibly reactionary, shackled—in their view—by the rhythms and forms of the nineteenth century? Or, could he have imagined that those composers would turn for inspiration to the works of his student Webern? Could he—could anyone—have foreseen that his sometime rival, Stravinsky, would suddenly adopt the twelve-tone method in the 1950s, stunning those who had regarded Stravinsky as the antithesis of serialism?

Far more than Schoenberg could ever have imagined or predicted, his twelve-tone idea has become one of the most influential ideas in the history of music. Of course, this is not to say that everyone has adopted Schoenberg's ideas—far from it. However, no one—composer, theorist, performer, historian, or critic—can properly come to terms with the music of this century without having to face Schoenberg's contribution. Indeed, the concepts Schoenberg discovered, the techniques he developed, the ideas he promulgated, and the methods he used have penetrated to every corner of our musical consciousness, transforming, irrevocably, our ideas of musical structure.

Surprisingly, notwithstanding the central importance of Schoenberg's twelve-tone method and the far-reaching influence of its ideas, very little attention has been devoted to examining the evolution of Schoenberg's technique, particularly from that critical period when he turned away from the contextual atonality of his pre-First World War compositions to the twelve-tone serialism of his works after 1920.

Yet, it is in those very compositions, the serial works from 1914–28, that Schoenberg's ideas changed so dramatically. Indeed, far from starting with a comprehensive view of the possibilities of serial organization, Schoenberg began with only the most tentative notion of the compositional potential of serialism. Then, with dogged persistence and merciless self-criticism, he gradually transformed his idea until it embraced every dimension of the musical fabric. It is that extraordinary transformation, that musical odyssey of discovery, that is the topic of this book.

No study such as this could come to fruition without the support and encouragement of many others. In particular I would like to thank the staff of the Arnold Schoenberg Institute—Leonard Stein, director, R. Wayne Shoaf, archivist, and the former archivist, Jerry McBride—for their generous help and assistance. During each of my three visits to the Institute they fulfilled my requests, answered all of my (countless) questions, and were always ready with whatever material or information I needed. I would also like to thank Claudio Spies of Princeton University for his thorough and critical reading of my typescript. His comments, criticisms, and suggestions for improvement have affected nearly every page in this book. I would also like to thank my colleague, Paul Johnson, who gave generously of his time and had many helpful suggestions. Finally, I wish to thank my wife for having the infinite patience to cope so cheerfully with a professor on sabbatical, at home for months on end, hunched over the word processor. Without her support this project would never have been started, let alone completed.

The preparation of the musical examples was made possible by a grant from the Institute for Scholarship in the Liberal Arts of the University of Notre Dame. A Summer Stipend from the National Endowment for the Humanities enabled me to bring this project to completion and is gratefully acknowledged.

E.H.

Acknowledgements

Grateful acknowledgement is due to the following for permission to reproduce extracts from the works cited:

Belmont Music Publishers, Los Angeles, California:

Die Jakobsleiter
Suite, Op. 25
Wind Quintet, Op. 26
Four Pieces for Mixed Choir, Op. 27
Three Satires, Op. 28
Suite, Op. 29
String Quartet No. 3
Variations for Orchestra, Op. 31
Von Heute auf Morgen, Op. 32
Klavierstück, Op. 33b
Prelude, Op. 44
Moses und Aron

Edition Wilhelm Hansen AS, Copenhagen:

Five Klavierstücke, Op. 23
Serenade, Op. 24

G. Schirmer Inc.:

Concerto for Violin, Op. 36
Fourth String Quartet, Op. 37

Extracts from the Arnold Schoenberg Gesamtausgabe are reproduced by courtesy of B. Schott's Söhne, Mainz

Facsimiles and Transcriptions of sketches and drafts are reproduced by courtesy of the Arnold Schoenberg Institute

Contents

I

The Twelve-tone Odyssey

> Today I have discovered something which will assure the supremacy of German music for the next hundred years.[1]

WITH this bit of characteristic if forgivable hyperbole, Arnold Schoenberg revealed to the world his new method of composition. The many resonances of this remark range from touching to ironic. In a little more than ten years Schoenberg would be a refugee, fleeing from a Germany embarked on a course of barbarism. German music, whose supremacy he had hoped to ensure, was destroyed as a vital force by the Nazis, who perverted the arts with their political and 'racial' ideology. The compositional method that Schoenberg thought would have such revolutionary impact achieved a degree of notoriety for a short time but then slipped from public attention. For a brief period after the Second World War the twelve-tone method was adopted by a number of composers, but today, only a handful follow Schoenberg's path.[2] It would seem that in every possible dimension his ecstatic vision has been proved wrong.

Yet, if one gauges the impact of the Schoenbergian revolution not in terms of its mass appeal to audiences or even to composers, but instead in terms of the value of its artistic legacy and the significance of ideas capable of further development, then one must accuse Schoenberg not of hyperbole, but of understatement. For he has left us with not only a precious inheritance of extraordinary twelve-tone compositions, but also with the answers to a wide range of the most difficult musical questions—questions that have faced those composers who chose, or felt compelled, to abandon tonality. That his compositions will continue to

---

[1] Josef Rufer asserts that Schoenberg made this statement to him towards the end of July 1921 during a stroll in Traunkirchen. See *The Works of Arnold Schoenberg*, trans. Dika Newlin (London, 1962), 45. However, Jan Maegaard suggests that the correct date might have been July 1922. Moreover, he presents evidence to show that Schoenberg probably first revealed his new idea to Erwin Stein and not to Rufer. See his *Studien zur Entwicklung des dodekaphonen Satzes bei Arnold Schönberg* (Copenhagen, 1972), i.96.

[2] Moreover, much of the post-war fascination with the twelve-tone idea stemmed from an interest, not in Schoenberg's works, but in those of Webern. Indeed, some of the most prominent participants in the avant-garde movement of the late 1940s and early 1950s even denied the revolutionary character of Schoenberg's thinking, seeing him mired in nineteenth-century modes of thought, particularly in the rhythmic domain. See Pierre Boulez, 'Schoenberg is Dead', *Score*, 6 (1952), 18–22.

be loved and admired by a small audience well beyond the 100 years mentioned by Schoenberg is something of which there should be little doubt. And, certainly, his ideas have already—directly and indirectly—transformed musical thought. Whether his compositional method will continue to influence composers is more problematic, depending partly on the extent to which his accomplishments are understood.

Such an understanding has been difficult to achieve, and for a variety of reasons. First and foremost is the truly revolutionary nature of Schoenberg's new system. The serial idea *was* something markedly different from its antecedents in a myriad of consequential ways. It fostered ways of thinking about musical organization that had been unimagined prior to Schoenberg's new method. As a result, some of the earliest writers and theorists had problems absorbing these new ideas. Some even tried to force this difficult music into the mould of tonality.[3] Others disseminated all kinds of misinformation about the system, with a range of 'rules' and 'exceptions' that bear little relation to the most significant features of Schoenberg's music.

Furthermore, Schoenberg, by nature secretive,[4] seems quite actively to have covered his tracks, emphasizing in his public statements the historical foundations of his new approach while minimizing the undeniable systematization of his compositional technique.[5] One can hardly blame Schoenberg for engaging in such self-protective tactics. He was subjected to a range of criticism and abuse that is shocking, even in hindsight. It should come as no surprise that in such an atmosphere Schoenberg did not reveal to the world the complicated technical procedures found in his music. It is only surprising that he revealed as much as he did. To have gone into details, to have revealed his compositional secrets would have opened himself to even more attacks and could have deflected attention permanently away from his music.

---

[3] A typical example is Paul Hindemith's harmonic analysis of Schoenberg's Op.33a: *The Craft of Musical Composition*, Book I, trans. Arthur Mendel (4th edn., New York, 1945), 217–19.

[4] Partly because of his secretive nature, Schoenberg's method was superficially understood, even by those in his circle. Consider, for example Rufer's monograph, *Composition with Twelve Tones*, trans. Humphrey Searle (New York, 1954). His description of Schoenberg's method contains little that could not be gleaned from Schoenberg's own writings on the subject.

[5] Schoenberg's most explicitly technical discussion of his twelve-tone method can be found in his essay, 'Composition with Twelve Tones (1)', in *Style and Idea*, ed. Leonard Stein, trans. Leo Black (New York, 1975), 214–45. An earlier version of this essay was given as a lecture at Princeton University. See his 'Vortrag/12 TK/Princeton', ed. Claudio Spies, *Perspectives of New Music*, 13 (1974), 58–136. In 'Composition with Twelve Tones' Schoenberg precedes the mildly technical discussion with a historical justification of his new method. He places his twelve-tone method in historical context as his answer to the problems posed by the abandonment of tonality. However, it is clear that Schoenberg had great reservations about publicly discussing his method. He feared—no doubt correctly—that an explicit and technical discussion of his method would lead to more accusations that he was a 'constructor' and not a real musician. See for example 'Vortrag', pp.118–23.

Finally, until recently most of Schoenberg's sketches and manuscripts were not available for study. As a result, the chronology of works from the critical period of the formation of the twelve-tone idea was not accurately known. Moreover, since theorists, interested in Schoenberg's music, did not have access to his sketches, they were unable to see the sketch material that often presents most explicitly the twelve-tone structures worked out in the music.

However, over the past thirty years, real progress has been made in the understanding of this music. In an important series of articles Milton Babbitt set forth the fundamental principles of the twelve-tone system and this has provided the stimulus for much productive work.[6] As a result theorists have been able to go far beyond simple note-counting and row-naming and have begun to suggest plausible answers to difficult questions of musical order and relatedness, progression and development. Furthermore, the opening of the Arnold Schoenberg Institute (1977) and the consequent availability of his manuscripts and sketches has opened whole new areas for study. In an important work, Jan Maegaard, primarily using material now at the Institute, clarified the chronology of Schoenberg's compositions, in particular those from the period of the formation of the serial idea.[7] Recently, as well, there have been a number of studies of Schoenberg's twelve-tone music using the treasure trove of sketch material found in the archives.[8] Given the powerful theoretical background provided by Babbitt and the possibilities opened by the availability of Schoenberg's sketches and manuscripts, we are now able to provide answers to substantive musical questions, both stylistic and analytic.

There is a further irony couched in Schoenberg's enthusiastic utterance. When he stated that he had discovered a method that would ensure the supremacy of German music for the next century, he was talking about his earliest serial compositions. We can easily understand his excitement, flush with enthusiasm over what must have seemed like a whole world of new compositional possibilities. Yet, over the next six to seven years virtually *every compositional characteristic* of those first serial works would be supplanted: Schoenberg had embarked on an odyssey of compositional discovery. He seems to have sensed that this particular route would take him closer to that elusive compositional goal for

[6] Babbitt's articles will be cited individually during the course of the book.

[7] Maegaard, 'A Study in the Chronology of op. 23–26 by Arnold Schoenberg', *Dansk aarbog for musikforskning*, 2 (1962), 93–115. Further information about the chronology of Schoenberg's works appears in Maegaard's *Studien*, i.

[8] Prominent among these are various writings of Martha Hyde. See her book *Schoenberg's Twelve-Tone Harmony*, (Ann Arbor, 1982), as well as the following articles: 'The Telltale Sketches: Harmonic Structure in Schoenberg's Twelve-Tone Method', *Musical Quarterly*, 66 (1980), 560–80 and 'The Format and Function of Schoenberg's Twelve-Tone Sketches', *Journal of the American Musicological Society*, 36 (1983), 453–80.

which he had been searching ever since Op.11. Thus, we might take his exclamation not so much as a eureka of final discovery but as a sign that he had found, at long last, the right direction.

When Schoenberg began this odyssey he faced a vast, previously unimagined, compositional world. In such circumstances it is hardly surprising that his early serial works display such a variety of approaches and solutions. Indeed, each of the compositions from Op.23 'fulfilled a uniquely innovatory stage in Schoenberg's voyage of compositional discovery'.[9] As he proceeded from composition to composition he tried a variety of different ways of manipulating his material. Yet for all the diversity and for all the stylistic change it is possible to discern a definite course in these wanderings. One by one in each of the compositions between Opp.23 and 32, there is the introduction and then the persistence of a number of compositional features. This is not evidence of aimless wandering, but rather of a sober critical process in which there was an active search for solutions to difficult compositional problems. By the time of the comic opera, *Von Heute auf Morgen*, Op.32, this process was virtually complete, and after that point changes in his compositional approach were not only fewer but far more circumscribed.

It has been stated that Schoenberg's music can be divided into three periods: chromatic tonal, atonal, and twelve-tone. But such a categorization, like the similar 'three periods' of Beethoven, obscures as much as it reveals. It is certainly true that in most of the compositions from 1920 to the end of his life Schoenberg employed his serial technique and, of course, it is also true that such serial techniques are not present in any real sense in either of the other two 'periods'.[10] None the less, the assertion that the twelve-tone period represents a stylistically unified body of works is simply not supported by the musical evidence.

Rather, during the first years of his serial period, Schoenberg, with unmatched patience and resolve, taught himself how to be a serial composer. During this period he methodically learned how to control a whole range of compositional features, from harmony to rhythm, form to set structure, developing variation to hexachordal progressions. And even though a process of experimentation and searching would always characterize his compositional approach, the solutions that Schoenberg found in this period remained the basis of his serial technique for the remainder of his career.

[9] Babbitt, 'Three Essays on Schoenberg', in Benjamin Boretz and Edward Cone (edd.), *Perspectives on Schoenberg and Stravinsky* (rev. edn., New York, 1972), 53.

[10] Occasional attempts to demonstrate serial procedures in Schoenberg's pre-serial compositions have revealed very little that can be thought of as serial in any meaningful sense of the word. See for example Rudolf Wille, 'Reihentechnik in Schönbergs op 19, 2', *'Die Musikforschung*, 19 (1966), 42–3.

As we follow Schoenberg along this odyssey, retracing his course, it is possible to gain a deeper understanding not only of this transitional period but of his mature style as well.[11] Such a period of stylistic development is a unique laboratory. In it we are given an opportunity to understand Schoenberg's compositional process as well as his own mechanisms for self-criticism. When Schoenberg drops one method of manipulating his material and substitutes another, we can do far more than identify the time and place of this change. We can delve into the underlying compositional reasoning, speculate about the features he found unsatisfactory in the discarded approach, and offer educated hypotheses about the compositional significance of the change. If it were the case that only one or two features changed during Schoenberg's formation of his mature twelve-tone style then this would be a rather unrewarding enterprise, based on little information. Such is hardly the case. The process of stylistic change and growth, evident in the compositions from Opp. 23 to 32, cover a gamut of twelve-tone compositional features: the structure of the set, the choice of set forms for simultaneous statement, rhythm and metre, the nature of harmonic combination, formal organization, and the exploitation of invariants.

Except for a few hints, discussions of these stylistic changes are absent from Schoenberg's writings and public statements. However, the music itself, examined chronologically, shows a continuous and thoroughgoing process of stylistic development, the product of the most rigorous and merciless self-criticism. We are witness to a composer who carefully and systematically formed a highly integrated musical method, one based on the interrelationship of pitch and rhythm, harmony and melody, local structure and long-range development, set structure and large-scale form. Schoenberg arrived at this refined stage only after a long and arduous compositional voyage, starting with the tentative efforts of Opp. 23 and 24, proceeding through the works of the 1920s, with each step gathering skill, power, and depth.

It may seem odd to describe Schoenberg's early serial compositions as tentative. After all, when Schoenberg began composing 'with twelve tones related only to one another' he was already nearly fifty years of age, with a wealth of compositional experience. This was the composer of the String Quartets, Opp. 7 and 10, the *Gurrelieder*, *Pierrot Lunaire*, the *Kammersymphonie*, Op. 9, and many other masterpieces. None the less, in 1921 Schoenberg was a novice as a serial composer. He was in the process of inventing a method of composition that had not, as yet, even been imagined. He could not possibly have been expected to see all at once the whole range of powerful compositional tools that were even-

[11] I use the term 'style' with the following carefully limited meaning: the specific or characteristic manner of execution, construction, and design.

tually to become the hallmarks of his mature twelve-tone style. He had set out on a lonely compositional odyssey with nothing but his own imagination to light the way. That he persisted through the first difficult period is a testament to both the persuasiveness of his vision and the indomitable nature of his spirit. That the eventual results include masterpieces like *Moses und Aron* should vindicate his perseverance.

2

Schoenberg's Mature Twelve-tone Style

THE most effective way to understand the individual stages in Schoenberg's formation and refinement of his twelve-tone method is to start not at the beginning of his complicated search but at the end, with a consideration of the properties of the mature twelve-tone style itself. Such a review will then permit us to look back at the transitional period and see Schoenberg's compositional choices in context, as components of a developing critical process, and not as a succession of unrelated decisions.

The formation of Schoenberg's mature twelve-tone style was not sudden, taking place between two consecutive works. Rather, there was a gradual process of trial and error, correction and refinement. Features introduced in one composition permitted the development of other, related characteristics in the next.

Therefore, it would be misleading to separate Schoenberg's mature twelve-tone works from their predecessors with an inflexible boundary. Moreover, even within the mature period there is a variety of approaches: Schoenberg never ceased to grow and experiment.

None the less, even though no unequivocal line separates the early and mature serial works, and even though stylistic change occurs throughout his twelve-tone period, it is still most revealing to think of Schoenberg's twelve-tone career as containing a mature period that begins with *Von Heute auf Morgen*, Op. 32, and includes the remaining twelve-tone compositions. These works form a coherent stylistic period because they share significant features that affect all dimensions of the musical fabric. Furthermore, many of the most prominent techniques of the early serial compositions are abandoned by Op. 32.

Not every work from the mature period contains every one of the features to be described below, but as a general rule a majority are present in the twelve-tone works from Opp. 32–50. The Variations for Orchestra, Op. 31, and the String Quartet No. 3, Op. 30, though they have many, even most, of the traits of the mature period, still possess enough of the characteristics of the earlier period that it is better to think of them as part of the process of transition, indeed, the very end of that process.

By no means should the impression be left that the following description of the properties of Schoenberg's mature twelve-tone style is presented as definitive or exhaustive. We have not learned enough about this music to be so presumptuous. None the less, given current knowledge of Schoenberg's use of the twelve-tone system, the following survey is comprehensive, dealing with salient features that have central roles in the structure of the music.

Although most of these features have been described individually, no study has shown their particular applicability, as a group, to the works after Op.31. Therefore, throughout this chapter, emphasis will be placed, not so much on a theoretical formulation of these characteristics but, rather, on their specific function in Schoenberg's mature twelve-tone compositions.

HEXACHORDAL INVERSIONAL COMBINATORIALITY

Few properties characteristic of Schoenberg's twelve-tone music have received as much attention as hexachordal inversional combinatoriality (IH-combinatoriality), and justifiably so, for it would be difficult to conceive of another property more fundamental in importance. Schoenberg himself, in his article 'Composition with Twelve Tones', gave some hints both to the significance of this concept and to the relatively late date of its appearance as a regular feature of his style.[1] Perhaps more than any other aspect of Schoenberg's twelve-tone music, this compositional idea has been generalized, extrapolated, and applied both in compositions and compositional theory.[2] Furthermore,

---

[1] 'Composition With Twelve Tones (1)', in *Style and Idea*, ed. Leonard Stein, trans. Leo Black (New York, 1975), 236. Schoenberg remarks that for the set of the Variations for Orchestra 'by making some slight changes, [I] built the basic set so that its antecedent, starting a minor third below, inverted itself into the remaining six tones of the full chromatic scale.' Schoenberg's association of the Variations for Orchestra with the introduction of IH-combinatoriality is fairly accurate. As we shall see, various aspects of this idea were formed during the period 1920–4. The first composition systematically to use IH-combinatoriality in a manner approaching that of the mature compositions was the little cantata, *Der neue Klassizismus* of Nov.–Dec. 1925. The Variations for Orchestra (originally the Passacaglia for Orchestra), were begun no later than Mar. 1926.

[2] IH-combinatoriality and the six all-combinatorial hexachords were described and discussed by Milton Babbitt in 'Some Aspects of Twelve-Tone Composition', *Score*, 12 (1955), 53–61. In a later article Babbitt discussed the properties of semi-combinatorial hexachords—not only IH-combinatoriality, but R- and RI-combinatoriality as well. In addition he mentioned other kinds of combinatoriality—trichordal, tetrachordal, etc.—demonstrating this with an example from one of his compositions. See his 'Set Structure as a Compositional Determinant', *Journal of Music Theory*, 5 (1961), 72–94. A good general description of combinatoriality is given by George Perle in *Serial Composition and Atonality* (5th edn., Los Angeles, 1981), 96–101. Perle notes that combinatoriality is characteristic of Schoenberg's music, but not that of Berg or Webern (p. 100). Babbitt's work in particular has been the inspiration for a number of interesting studies about combinatoriality and aggregate formation. See Donald Martino, 'The Source Set and Its Aggregate Formations', *Journal of Music Theory*, 5 (1961), 224–73; Daniel Starr and Robert Morris, 'A General Theory of Combinatoriality and the Aggregate', *Perspectives of New Music*, 16/1 (1977), 3–35 (Part 1) and *Perspectives of New Music*, 16 (1978), 50–84 (Part 2); Starr, 'Derivation and Polyphony', *Per-*

IH-combinatoriality has such a profound influence on so many other compositional features—harmonic structure, aggregate rhythm, hexachordal levels, degrees of relatedness—that an understanding of its use in Schoenberg's mature style is a prerequisite for the understanding of those features as well.

Hexachordal inversional combinatoriality is a property:

as a result of which any one of the two disjunct hexachords of any of the, at most, 48 set forms can be associated with the order corresponding hexachord of one or more inversions of that set form transposed by an interval or intervals determined by the pitch class ordering of the pitch classes within the hexachord, so that each such pair of hexachords contains all twelve pitch classes.[3]

For example, the opening set form (P-0) of Schoenberg's Fourth String Quartet, Op. 37, is D C♯ A B♭ F D♯/E C A♭ G F♯ B. The inversionally related set form whose hexachords have no pitch-class intersection with the corresponding hexachords of P-0 is I-5: G A♭ C B E F♯/ F A C♯ D E♭ B♭. Thus each pair of order corresponding hexachords contains all twelve pitch classes. The first time these set forms occur together in the composition is in m. 27 where the hexachords are counterpointed against one another, each pair lasting precisely two beats (see Ex. 2.1). Thus, each half measure contains all twelve pitch classes (cf. 'Aggregate', below).

Schoenberg's mature handling of IH-combinatoriality was dependent on far more than just the IH-combinatorial property of the set. Indeed, most of Schoenberg's early twelve-tone works used IH-combinatorial sets. However, in those compositions one or more of the characteristics of the mature approach were absent: although the set might be IH-combinatorial in structure it was not subdivided into hexachords (e.g. Op. 25); a set, even though IH-combinatorial, and even though subdivided into hexachords, was not combined with that particular transformation of the forty-eight forms that produces aggregates between order corresponding hexachords (e.g. Op. 26); a set, even though IH-combinatorial, subdivided into hexachords, and conjoined with the appropriate transformation, is not rhythmically aligned with that transformation so as to produce aggregates (e.g. Op. 27 No. 1).

These are precisely the features that are of such central importance in the mature style. In nearly all of the twelve-tone compositions after Op. 30 Schoenberg not only uses a set that is IH-combinatorial in structure, but also makes the hexachordal subdivision the normative articulation of the set, associates a given set form with its IH-combinatorially

spectives of New Music, 23 (1984), 180–257. Finally, for a German language summary of Babbitt's ideas on combinatoriality, the aggregate, and invariants, see Eberhardt Klemm, 'Zur Theorie der Reihenstruktur und Reihendisposition in Schönbergs 4. Streichquartette', *Beiträge zur Musikwissenschaft*, 8 (1966), 27–49.

[3] Babbitt, 'Set Structure', pp. 129–30.

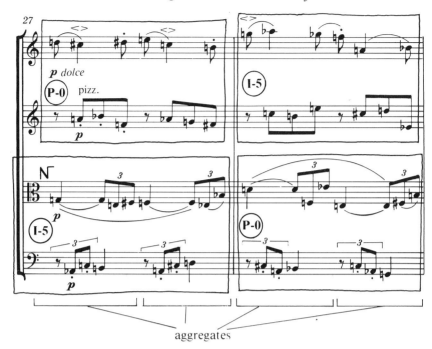

Ex. 2.1 Fourth String Quartet, Op. 37, mm. 27–8: IH-combinatoriality

P-O: D C♯ A B♭ F D♯ / E C A♭ G F♯ B
I-5: G A♭ C B E F♯ / F A C♯ D E♭ B♭

related counterpart, and when those forms are associated, is careful to align the order corresponding hexachords to produce aggregates.

Therefore, in the mature compositions, the only way two set forms occur simultaneously is in IH-combinatorial pairs. Effectively, no other method of set combination exists: either a set is stated by itself, partitioned into several voices, or it is stated together with its inversionally related, aggregate forming, combinatorial partner. This consistency has profound implications, particularly for harmonic structure (cf. 'Harmony', below).

In addition to setting norms for polyphonic combination, Schoenberg uses the property of IH-combinatoriality to determine local set choice. Often, sections of music are characterized by a circumscribed group of set forms: he limits set choice within sections to those four forms that constitute an IH-combinatorial complex (cf. 'Hexachordal levels' below).

Moreover, by placing in temporal succession two IH-combinatorially related set forms, arranged so as to conjoin their pitch-class complementary hexachords, aggregates are formed. For example, in the first six measures of the third movement of Op.37, a linear, unison statement of P-o is followed immediately with a statement of RI-5. The juxtaposition of the second hexachord of P-o (D B♭ G♭ F E A) with the first hexachord of RI-5 (A♭ D♭ C B G D♯) produces an aggregate.[4]

By contrast, when the conjoined hexachords of two successively stated IH-combinatorial set forms are not pitch-class complementary, but pitch-class equivalent, no aggregate is formed. This preservation of content, but not of order, permits us to hear the second hexachord as a reordered variant of its predecessor. This is an important component of Schoenberg's manipulation of the properties of the set for the purposes of developing variation.

AGGREGATES

The creation of aggregates by the association of order corresponding hexachords of IH-combinatorially related set forms is but a single manifestation of the more general procedure of aggregate formation, a feature that lies at the heart of Schoenberg's mature twelve-tone style. The formation of aggregates is achieved in a variety of ways in Schoenberg's works, not only involving immediate relationships between and within sets, but also extending to a middleground level. The pervasive appearance of aggregates as fundamental units of musical structure in Schoenberg's works is an aspect whose central importance must not be underestimated.[5]

In some ways the aggregate might be understood to be prior to the twelve-tone set, both historically and systematically. Chronologically it must be remembered that chromatic completion, the antecedent of the aggregate, preceded the twelve-tone set as a compositional construct. Moreover, it is evident from Schoenberg's own comments that the twelve-tone set—at least in its initial stages—evolved from his attempts to systematize the circulation of the twelve pitch classes.[6]

At the same time, the aggregate, in a general, systematic sense, is an overall concept—any collection of the twelve pitch classes without regard to order—that subsumes specific, compositionally expressed presentations of the twelve pitch classes: the set, secondary sets, as well as

---

[4] When the elements forming aggregates of this sort are presented successively this is termed a 'secondary set'. See Babbitt, 'Some Aspects', p.57.

[5] The central importance of aggregate formation, and its many implications for Schoenberg's music and beyond are discussed in Babbitt, 'Since Schoenberg', *Perspectives of New Music*, 12 (1973–4), 3–28.

[6] As Schoenberg remarked: 'The construction of a basic set of twelve tones derives from the intention to postpone the repetition of every tone as long as possible'. See 'Composition with Twelve Tones (2)', *Style and Idea*, p.246.

the aggregate in the compositional sense.[7] The all-pervasiveness of aggregates at both foreground and middleground levels, is an indication of both Schoenberg's conscious understanding of the centrality of this concept and his recognition of the systematic connections between explicit presentations of the set and the compositionally expressed aggregates to which they relate.[8]

Ex. 2.1 demonstrated one type of aggregate formation, specifically that which results from the juxtaposition of order corresponding hexachords of IH-combinatorially related set forms. The examples that follow should give some indication of the diversity of aggregate formation in this music.

Schoenberg based his one-act opera, *Von Heute auf Morgen*, Op. 32, on a set that employs two different orderings of the final hexachord. In mm. 25–6 the two IH-combinatorially related set forms I-3 and P-t appear in succession, each lasting one measure (see Ex. 2.2).

Ex. 2.2 displays two levels of aggregate structure. On the most local level each of the two partitioned set forms is an aggregate—in an ordering significant for this piece, but an aggregate none the less. On a higher level aggregates are created by elements grouped together by rhythm, timbre, and order number. In m. 25 the pitches in the voice, F and D, combined with those in the oboe, E B♭ F♯ G♯, form one hexachord and this is complemented by the functionally equivalent material in m. 26, producing an aggregate. At the same time, the material in the strings, harp, and horn forms another aggregate.

The formation, as in Ex. 2.2, of aggregates spanning several local set

---

[7] The distinction between the aggregate in the compositional and systematic senses was made by Babbitt in 'Set Structure', p. 140. Unfortunately, there has developed a certain imprecision in the use of the term aggregate. It has been used not only to describe an unordered collection of twelve pitches with no pitch class repeated but, also, to refer to any collection that includes all twelve pitch classes, regardless of repetitions. Babbitt made a careful distinction between aggregates (one instance of each pitch class) and weighted aggregates ('a collection of twelve pitches in which the twelfth pitch does not appear until after, at least, one pitch class has been represented, at least, twice, with each of these representations supplied by segments of different set forms'). See 'Set Structure', p. 138. In this book, the term 'aggregate' will be carefully reserved for an unordered (or, in the case of a partitioned set, a partially ordered) collection of twelve pitch classes— without duplications. For a collection containing all twelve pitch classes, but with duplications, the term 'chromatic completion' will be used. The use of this general term (as distinct from the very specific term 'weighted aggregate') is necessary to account for those numerous passages from Schoenberg's early serial period in which the informal inclusion of all twelve tones, without regard for repetitions, was a prominent feature, and where the repeated pitch classes were not necessarily elements of different set forms.

[8] I use the term 'middleground aggregate' to refer to an aggregate that is formed from elements of at least two local set forms. Thus there are two levels of structure: a level formed of local set statements and a higher level subsuming elements from those local statements. The derivation of the term is, of course, from Schenkerian theory. Others have suggested similar parallels between twelve-tone theory and Schenkerian ideas. See Babbitt, 'Set Structure', p. 138 where he uses the term 'middleground harmonic structure' to denote harmonic structures situated 'hierarchically between the "foreground" structure of simultaneities and their relations, and the larger areas including and subsuming aggregates as their constituents.'

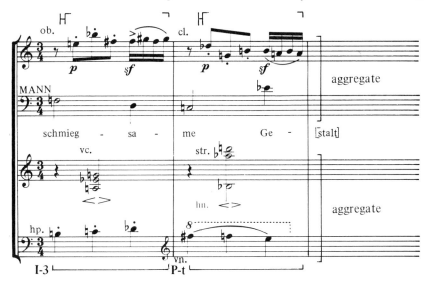

Ex. 2.2 *Von Heute auf Morgen*, mm. 25–6: aggregates spanning successive set statements

I-3: F E Bb F♯ G♯ D / B C Eb G A Db
P-t: C Db G B A Eb / F♯ F D Bb Ab E

forms, shows the way in which this feature can extend past the foreground to exert control over longer spans of musical time. The constituent elements take on two structural roles: on the surface they function as elements of each local set form; over a longer span of time these same elements contribute to the unfolding aggregate. Here are the fundamental building-blocks of twelve-tone hierarchy, with both local detail and longer-range structures derived from and relating back to a common systematic origin.

Another passage from *Von Heute auf Morgen*, mm. 335–8, demonstrates how aggregate formation can extend past two local set forms (see Ex. 2.3). In these four measures the following set forms appear at the local level: P-o, R-o, RI-5, and I-5 (all ordering variants). Of particular interest is the vocal part. In each measure the voice states three pitch classes and, in total, over the four measures, all twelve pitch classes are represented. This aggregate is the unifying musical structure that binds these measures together into one large musical unit. It is neither inconsequential, nor accidental that this aggregate unfolds in the vocal part, for this is but one way that Schoenberg asserts the hierarchical priority of that line. Moreover, the first six pitch classes of the voice part, and thus the last six as well, form pitch-class set 023468, the hexachord of the set, and this hexachord is at the same transpositional level as the accompanying local set forms.

Ex. 2.3 *Von Heute auf Morgen*, mm. 335–8: aggregate, vocal part, unfolding over four local setstatements

P-o (variant): D E♭ A C♯ B F C B♭ A♭ G F♯ E
I-5 (variant): G F♯ C A♭ B♭ E A B C♯ D E♭ F

Any assessment of the role of aggregates in Schoenberg's mature twelve-tone music must take into consideration the consistency with which aggregates mark off the flow of time. The following example, from the Concerto for Violin, presents a typical situation (see Ex. 2.4). A succession of aggregates divides the time line, and this subdivision is exhaustive, leaving no span of time that is not part of an aggregate's temporal domain. As a result, the aggregate is a periodic and reiterative compositional construct, and the only such construct that saturates the compositional surface. The implications of this for metric structure are profound, and will be taken up later (cf. 'Metre', below).

LINEAR SET PRESENTATION

The straightforward linear-thematic presentation of the set is by no means the customary method of stating the set. Indeed, in most of the mature twelve-tone works, such linear set statements are relatively rare and are reserved for points of important structural, or, as in *Moses und Aron*, musical/dramatic emphasis.

In most of the mature works a clearly etched linear-thematic presentation of the set appears at the very beginning of the composition. Sometimes, however, as in the Variations for Orchestra, Op.31, the first linear presentation is deferred by a well-defined introduction.

Schoenberg's custom of presenting a linear statement of the set as a theme and placing that theme at the beginning of the work is a crucial feature of the developmental process in his compositions. A linear set statement presents the referential material in an unambiguous ordering. Therefore, subsequent partitioned set statements must be understood to flow from and relate to this fundamental referential idea. By beginning his compositions with the set stated as a line, Schoenberg establishes a focus for subsequent developments.

In several of his works, particularly more extended ones, the initial linear presentation includes not only P-o, but all or most of those forms that make up the referential IH-combinatorial complex. By so doing, Schoenberg presents both the fundamental referential thematic material and the norms of set combination and association.

After the initial statement of the set, further linear statements tend to be reserved for the articulation of important structural points. This is usually accomplished by a restatement of the referential material, often at a new transpositional level. The first movement of the Fourth String Quartet offers a number of characteristic examples. After the opening linear statements of the IH-combinatorial complex (mm. 1–23) no further linear presentations of the set occur for the next forty measures. Then, in m. 63, coincidental with a dramatic change in texture, timbre, surface rhythm, and tempo, Schoenberg states I-o as a line in the first

Ex. 2.4 Concerto for Violin, Op. 36, mm. 151–7: the time line as a succession
of aggregates

violin. This acts to close the previous section and prepare a section in which a new theme is accompanied by a variant of the opening theme of the quartet. In mm. 69–78 there are linear statements of the set forms from this new IH-combinatorial complex (I-0, R-7, RI-0). Throughout the movement the initiation of new sections is marked and confirmed by clear linear presentations of the set (mm. 95, 165, 178, and 192).

In *Moses und Aron* the presentation of the set in a straightforward, linear manner is a rare occurrence and its use is reserved for points of exceptional musical/dramatic significance. The first entrance of Aron is the first time in the opera that the set is stated in a linear-thematic manner, and in some important senses this marks the beginning of the opera's action. At this point Aron sings, in succession, linear statements of those set forms that make an IH-combinatorial complex (Act I, mm. 124–45). Moses, who throughout the opera presents his material in *Sprechstimme*, is given but one opportunity for normal singing, and at this point (Act I, mm. 208–14), with the words 'Reinige dein Denken', his melody is a linear statement of the set.[9]

PARTITIONING

Given the relative rarity of purely linear set presentations, it follows that polyphonic partitioning is the norm. The use of such partitioned sets can pose a number of interesting compositional challenges. Whereas a linear statement presents the set in a manner that does not violate or obscure the referential interval ordering, a partitioned set normally results in the creation of secondary set relationships: lines or chords whose elements may not represent consecutive order positions in the referential set.[10] This produces explicit relationships between non-adjacent elements of the set.[11] In Schoenberg's mature works partitioning became a precision tool, whereby secondary set relationships were exploited systematically, with a profound effect on many compositional dimensions, from local harmony, to long-range development.

[9] Babbitt, 'Three Essays on Schoenberg', in Benjamin Boretz and Edward Cone (edd.), *Perspectives on Schoenberg and Stravinsky* (rev. edn., New York, 1972), 56–7.

[10] Strictly speaking a linear statement of a set is the 12^1 partitioning. However, throughout this book a linear statement of a set is not referred to as a 'partitioned' set form. Many of the theoretical issues that relate to the problem of generating polyphony from a linear referential idea are discussed in Peter Westergaard, 'Toward a Twelve-Tone Polyphony', *Perspectives of New Music*, 4 (1966), 90–112.

[11] For instance, if a set is partitioned into vertical trichords as follows:

$$0 \quad 3 \quad 6 \quad 9$$
$$1 \quad 4 \quad 7 \quad t$$
$$2 \quad 5 \quad 8 \quad e$$

then the succession in the top voice (order numbers 0369) does not represent a segment from the set.

The association of pitch classes, not so associated in the referential set, can present fruitful avenues for development. By such means harmonies of the set can be outlined, future regions suggested, and past references confirmed.[12]

In his early twelve-tone works, as we shall see, Schoenberg tended to partition the set into discrete equal segments, either linearly, vertically, or both. And, indeed, partitioning the set into discrete, equal units was not limited to Schoenberg's early twelve-tone works. To the contrary, it appeared throughout his twelve-tone career (see for instance mm. 45–7 in the first movement of the Fourth String Quartet). Yet, there are some limitations to this kind of partitioning, limitations Schoenberg dropped in his mature twelve-tone style.

Partitioning into equal segments dictates that all the partitioned secondary lines be of equal size. This has the effect of permitting the secondary line to be formed from one and only one element from each discrete segment. For example, within a secondary line, an order-number succession of 01679 would be impossible when partitioning is limited to discrete equal segments of the set. Such limitations have a substantial impact on the kinds of secondary relationships that can be formed. In Schoenberg's mature twelve-tone works there is a more varied use of partitioning and it is employed to produce powerful compositional relationships. A selection from the Concerto for Violin, Op. 36 (mm. 83–4), offers a good example of Schoenberg's use of partitioning in a mature work (see Ex. 2.5). In this example, Schoenberg has partitioned P-5 into four voices. The solo violin states order positions 2 5 7 t, the first violins 1 3 8 e. Order positions 0 and 6 appear in the cellos and basses while the horn presents order positions 4 and 9. Thus, unlike the norm in the early serial works, the partitioned segments are of different sizes—in this case, either four elements or two. Within the four lines not one adjacency is preserved from the referential set. Or, to put it another way, every compositionally associated, linear adjacency conjoins elements not adjacent in the set.

This is not to say that the referential set bears an arbitrary relationship to the compositional surface—far from it. Order precedence is not violated and, as a result, the attacked simultaneities represent segments of the set. For example, the trichord A G♯ E, struck on the last beat of m. 83, spans order positions 2–4 of the set. Similarly, the trichord C♯ G B♭ (at the end of the excerpt) contains order positions 9–e of the set.

The conjunction, on the compositional surface, of elements not ad-

---

[12] Much attention has been paid to the relationship of partitioned segments to the structure of the set. See particularly Martha Hyde, *Schoenberg's Twelve-Tone Harmony* (Ann Arbor, 1982). This book, and its related articles will be discussed in detail in footnotes to the section on Harmony below.

Ex. 2.5 Concerto for Violin: 4, 4, 2, 2 partitioning of P-5

P-5: D E♭ G♯ E A B / F F♯ C C♯ G B♭

jacent in the referential set, presents Schoenberg with an opportunity
to exploit the associations formed by these specific secondary relationships. Thus it can be seen that partitioning can direct the developmental progression, and as such can be one of the principal determinants of
local association, set succession and, therefore, formal differentiation as
well.[13] An analysis of the function of the secondary set relationships in
Ex. 2.5 should give some hint of the enormous compositional potential
that results from the manipulation of these relationships.

   The succession in the first violins, E♭ E C B♭, represents order positions 1 3 8 e from the set. This association of order numbers is hardly
casual, for the resultant pitch-class set is 0146, a pitch-class set embedded within the twelve-tone set at order-positions 4–7. Any non-symmetrical tetrachord, of a given content, will appear only that number
of times among the twenty-four prime and inversional transformations
of the set as that pitch-class set is embedded within the set. In the
present case pitch-class set 0146 (a non-symmetrical tetrachord) is
embedded in the set only once, at order positions 4–7, and, therefore,
there is one and only one set in which these specific pitch classes, E♭ E C
B♭, appear as a segment: I-t. Of course, I-t is the IH-combinatorial
counterpart to P-5 and appears throughout this section of the work.
Given strict ordering, the segment E♭ E C B♭, must appear as a literal
set segment in every statement of I-t (see mm. 84–5 and 86–7, where

---

[13] Relationships of this sort were first pointed out by Babbitt. See 'Set Structure', p. 141, where
he shows how the dyads A-B♭ and D-E in mm. 621–2 of the Fourth String Quartet were 'compositionally secured' through the instrumental partitioning.

this tetrachord occurs with the elements in close proximity). Moreover, in m. 91, Schoenberg states set forms P-5 and I-t subdivided into vertical tetrachords. Since pitch-class set 0146 is embedded in the set at order positions 4–7—one of the disjunct tetrachords—it follows that E♭ E C B♭ must occur as the middle tetrachord in any tetrachordally segmented statement of I-t.[14]

The use of secondary set structures, created by partitioning, to foster compositional associations between different set forms, is a fundamental aspect of Schoenberg's mature twelve-tone technique. By such means local set successions are regulated, future areas adumbrated, past references confirmed. In a very real sense, then, the specific partitionings used can shape the direction of the development. Schoenberg employs this technique not merely to associate two local set forms, but also to determine the progression from one IH-combinatorial complex to the next and thus structure the large-scale choice of set forms. From this it can be inferred that the large-scale form of Schoenberg's mature twelve-tone works is related to and develops from the local partitioning. One particularly clear example should help illustrate Schoenberg's control of this dimension.

The Prelude, Op.44, uses only three IH-combinatorial complexes: IH-combinatorial complex 0 (i.e. P-0, I-5, R-0, RI-5, hereafter abbreviated, CC-0), CC-5, and CC-7. As is typical of many of Schoenberg's mature twelve-tone works, the set forms used in the first section of the composition (mm. 1–24) are limited to CC-0. This complex, by its temporal position and durational emphasis, should be understood as a referential region (cf. 'Hexachordal levels', below). Then, in m. 25, concurrent with a dramatic change in timbre, volume, density, and tempo, a new section begins, characterized by a new partitioning of the set and a new IH-combinatorial complex, CC-5 (see Ex. 2.6). Both P-5 and RI-t are partitioned identically (cf. 'Isomorphic Partitioning', below) with the upper voice stating order positions 0134, 679t, and the lower voice order positions 25, 8e. Immediately following, in m. 30, Schoenberg moves to a new IH-combinatorial complex, CC-7. Here too he states the material using this partitioning. From this point until m. 65, the CC-5 and CC-7 regions alternate, with consistent use made of the 0134, 679t, 258e partitioning.

At m. 65 Schoenberg returns to CC-0, but this time the partitioning, introduced in m. 25 and applied to CC-5 and CC-7, is finally stated in CC-0. The choice of set forms, their temporal placement, the partition-

---

[14] In the isomorphically partitioned statement of I-t, mm. 86–7, there is a deviation from the referential ordering. According to the set the B♭ in the violin in m. 87 should be a B. Undoubtedly the B♭ is a mistake and should be corrected. See my 'Editing Schoenberg's Twelve-Tone Music', *Journal of the Arnold Schoenberg Institute*, 8 (1984), 141–57 for a discussion of these issues.

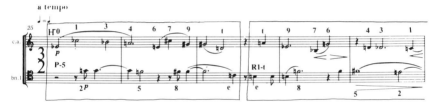

Ex. 2.6 Prelude, Op. 44: the opening of the section, beginning at m. 25 with the partitioning 0134, 679t, 258e

ings, as well as the structure of the set itself, are a group of interrelated features that together contribute to the articulation of the form.

The return of CC-0 at m. 65 with the partitioning of Ex. 2.6 has been prepared by the prior application of that partitioning to CC-5 and CC-7. This follows from the intervallic characteristics of the partitioned tetrachords coupled with these particular combinations of set forms.

The partitioned tetrachords in the upper parts are pitch-class sets 0126 and 0137 respectively. At the same time, the lower tetrachord, spanning the two discrete hexachords, is pitch-class set 0127. Each of these three partitioned tetrachords has at least one three-element subset in common with each of the other two tetrachords. Therefore, the combination of CC-5 and CC-7, in this specific partitioning, functions to prepare the return of CC-0. When CC-0 finally appears with this partitioning it has been prepared by the common subsets, coupled with the complementary transpositional levels. As a result, every partitioned tetrachord of CC-0 has three pitch classes in common with at least one partitioned tetrachord from either CC-5 or CC-7 (see Ex. 2.7). In several instances the common pitch classes remain in their original registral relationship, highlighting the connection (see Ex. 2.8).

Thus, in Op. 44 the specific content of the sections is dependent on the interaction of the structure of the set and the local partitioning.

P-5		RI-t	
Eb B Bb A	E C# G# D	A Eb Bb G	D C# C G#
G F	F# C	B F	F# E

P-0		I-5	
Bb Gb F E	B G# Eb A	Eb G G# A	D F Bb E
D C	Db G	B C#	C F#

I-0		R-7	
Bb D Eb E	A C F B	E Bb Eb F#	B C C# F
F# G#	G C#	D G#	G A

Ex. 2.7 Prelude, Op. 44: common tone preparation for the partitioned tetrachords of P-0/I-5

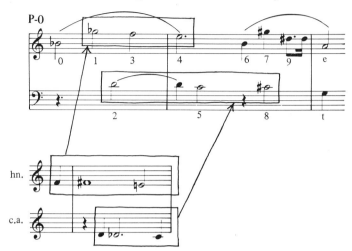

Ex. 2.8 Prelude, Op. 44, mm. 66–8 and 28–9: the preparation of P-0 in the
0134, 679t, 258e partitioning by registral invariance of common tones

Schoenberg chose CC-5 and CC-7 not merely because of immediately
obvious relationships between the linear orderings of the set forms but,
rather, because of relationships that result from a specific partitioning
applied to the set.

ISOMORPHIC PARTITIONING

Complementing the associative and developmental techniques made
possible by individual partitionings is Schoenberg's principal method
for the relation of partitioned set forms to one another: isomorphic partitioning.[15] This technique, in which two or more set forms are partitioned identically, was exploited by Schoenberg to create refined
invariant relationships. By virtue of its power and flexibility it became
one of the most important components of Schoenberg's twelve-tone
style.

The extraordinary pervasiveness of isomorphic partitioning in

[15] Schoenberg's use of isomorphic partitioning was described in Ethan Haimo and Paul Johnson, 'Isomorphic Partitioning and Schoenberg's Fourth String Quartet', *Journal of Music Theory*,
28 (1984), 47–72. Of course, Schoenberg never used the term 'isomorphic partitioning', nor for
that matter most of the terms in use today to describe his method. None the less, even though—as
far as we know—he never developed a theoretical vocabulary to describe his techniques there is
abundant evidence in his manuscripts that indicates just how concrete his understanding of those
ideas actually was. For example, preserved in the archives are a number of pieces of cardboard
with several little squares cut out. These pieces of cardboard conform precisely to the size of
Schoenberg's set tables. When placed over a given set form in a set table an extracted segment
would appear in the little windows. When the device was slid up or down to another set form,
another isomorphically partitioned segment would result. For details of a similar device used in
Moses und Aron, see Jan Maegaard, 'Schönbergs Zwölftonreihen', *Die Musikforschung* 29 (1976),
394.

Ex. 2.9 *Moses und Aron*, mm. 98–9: isomorphic partitioning

Schoenberg's mature twelve-tone works is a mark of the centrality of this technique. Although isomorphic partitioning is also a feature of Schoenberg's earliest serial compositions, it is an isolated procedure in those works. By contrast, in some of the mature twelve-tone works it is possible to find an isomorphic partitioning relationship for virtually every set presentation in the work.

The most common procedure is the isomorphic partitioning of two consecutive I-related set forms. This highlights interval-class relationships between the two forms. These relationships, like those with isomorphic partitioning applied to T-related set forms, are independent of any special features of the set. A characteristic example is provided by the opening of the second scene, Act I, of *Moses und Aron* (see Ex. 2.9). Here, in consecutive measures, Schoenberg states P-0 and I-3, partitioned according to an identical scheme.

The flute states order positions 4578 in both set forms; similarly, the harp presents order positions 23te and the violin order positions 0169. The most immediately perceptible consequence of this fixed order-number assignment is the equivalence of pitch-class sets formed by elements of like order number. For example, the pitch classes in the flute in m. 98, D♯ C♯ E♯ F♯ form pitch-class set 0135—equivalent to the pitch-class set in the flute in m. 99: F♯ G♯ E D♯.[16]

Moreover, given consistent assignment of duration and metric placement of the elements of isomorphically related set forms, all metrically equivalent vertical harmonies will be held invariant as well. In m. 98

[16] For a full discussion of the concept of equivalent pitch-class sets see Alan Forte, *The Structure of Atonal Music* (New Haven and London, 1973).

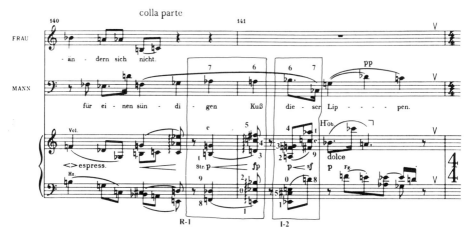

Ex. 2.10 *Von Heute auf Morgen*, mm. 140–1: isomorphic partitioning of RI-related set forms—order of operations: isomorphic partitioning first, retro-grade second

the first vertical trichord consists of pitch classes D♯, E, and A: pitch-class set 016, a trichord that, incidentally, is equivalent to the opening trichord of the set (cf. 'Harmony', below). Given equivalent durations and metric placement the comparable sonority in m. 99, F♯ G C, is—necessarily—also a 016 trichord. Similar results can be obtained by comparing metrically equivalent points in the two measures.

Isomorphic partitioning occurs most often between successive I-related sets. Schoenberg's preference for this kind of partitioning is underlined by the way isomorphic partitioning is applied to RI-related set forms. When successive set forms are RI-related Schoenberg gener-ally applies isomorphic partitioning first and then retrograde. For in-stance, in Schoenberg's *Von Heute auf Morgen*, Op.32, the following passage occurs in mm. 140–1 (see Ex. 2.10). In this example a state-ment of R-1 is followed by I-2. If both are assigned order numbers 0–e with the R-form's numbers descending from eleven, then the isomor-phic character of the partitioning is clear. Since this kind of partition-ing (as opposed to true RI-isomorphic partitioning) is by far the most common type, the convention has been adopted throughout this book of assigning descending order numbers to R- and RI-forms. In the few cases where true R- or RI-isomorphic partitioning takes place this would be seen by the complementation (to eleven) of order numbers.[17]

One measure of the importance of isomorphic partitioning in Schoenberg's mature twelve-tone compositions is its pervasiveness. It

---

[17] That is, the complement of order number 0 is e, of order number 1 is t, of order number 2 is 9, etc.

appears in every one of the mature compositions, sometimes effecting virtually every measure. Moreover, examples of all possible types of iso-morphic partitioning are found in his twelve-tone works: inversional, retrograde, retrograde-inversional, and transpositional.

Invariant pitch-class sets like those seen in Ex. 2.9 occur between any two isomorphically partitioned, I-related sets; these invariants are not dependent on any feature of the set's ordering or on the particular par-titioning. However, beyond these general compositional relationships, Schoenberg also actively sought to create pitch-class invariance of par-titioned segments. Invariants of this sort are dependent not only on the specific partitioning but on the transpositional level chosen for the iso-morphically partitioned form (see Ex. 2.11). For example, in m. 107 of the Variations for Orchestra, P-3 appears, partitioned between oboe and strings, with the oboe stating order positions 013578. Two measures later, in a statement of P-9, these same order positions appear in the flute. Since this partitioned segment contains three disjunct dyads, each a tritone, under T6 the content of the three dyads is held fixed.

Isomorphic partitioning of I-related set forms also plays a central role in Schoenberg's twelve-tone phrase structure. Isomorphic parti-tioning functions to articulate phrases by systematic intervallic re-lationships. Given a partitioned set form, followed by an isomorphically partitioned I-related form, it follows that as the second set form unfolds it replicates the interval succession of the first, creating a compelling logic of pattern completion. The phrase is complete when

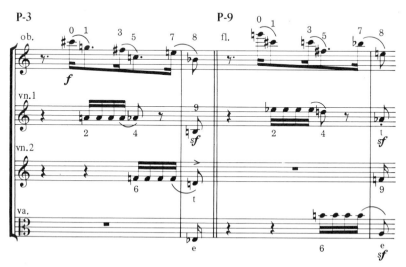

Ex. 2.11 Variations for Orchestra, mm. 107–8 and 109–10: invariance under isomorphic partitioning of T-related set forms

the internal interval patterns have been duplicated. Because these relationships are I-related with a fixed index number, it follows that all pairs of segments with identical order-number content form symmetrical pitch-class sets, and all such pitch-class sets have the same axis of symmetry.[18]

INVARIANTS

The formation and manipulation of invariants was one of the first serial procedures whose compositional significance Schoenberg recognized and exploited. From the very beginning of his serial period Schoenberg sought ways to relate different set forms to one another through invariants preserved under serial operations. Moreover, this feature—unlike many others from the first serial works—was not abandoned as Schoenberg's twelve-tone technique developed. Instead, its use was refined and polished and became a technique of ever greater power and subtlety.

Some invariant relationships are simply properties of the twelve-tone system—the invariance of interval-class succession under T is an obvious example—and demand no special ordering of the set or association of particular transformations to be operative.[19] However, from the first serial sketches, Schoenberg showed an interest in constructing sets so that at a particular transformation of that set some segment of the original would be held fixed in content, though not necessarily in order.[20]

This particular concept became a central criterion for determining degrees of relatedness among the forty-eight set forms. One obvious manifestation of this is Schoenberg's tendency, described above, to proceed by groups of IH-combinatorially related set forms (see Ex. 2.12). In this example, the opening measures of the Concerto for Violin, Op. 36, the opening set form P-0 proceeds immediately to I-5. In immediate succession, therefore, are two hexachords with the same pitch-class content. As a result, the first hexachord of I-5 relates to what has preceded it on two levels. On one level, of course, this hexachord must be understood as a transposed inversion of the first hexachord of P-0. The rhythm, contour, and phrase assignments underline this connection in the clearest possible terms. But, at the same time, on another

---

[18] For a definition and discussion of index number see Babbitt, 'Twelve-Tone Rhythmic Structure and the Electronic Medium', *Perspectives of New Music*, 1 (1962), 49–79.

[19] The definitive discussion of twelve-tone invariants is Babbitt, 'Twelve-Tone Invariants as Compositional Determinants', *Musical Quarterly*, 46 (1960), 246–59. Formalized procedures for identifying invariants are discussed in David Beach, 'Segmental Invariance and the Twelve-Tone System', *Journal of Music Theory*, 20(1976), 157–84

[20] An excellent discussion of Schoenberg's use of invariants can be found in David Lewin, 'A Theory of Segmental Association', *Perspectives of New Music*, 1 (1962), 89–116.

Ex. 2.12 Concerto for Violin: successive hexachords of identical pitch-class content

level, the pitch-class content of the first hexachord of I-5 may also be understood as a permutation of the content of the second hexachord of P-o.

This then is the essential, critical characteristic of Schoenberg's handling of invariants: at one and the same time a passage must be understood to relate in two (or more) ways to its antecedents. Neither by itself gives a complete picture; only taken together can they be understood in the richness of their relational constructs.

In addition to invariants preserved between two set forms Schoenberg exploited invariants that result from the combination of forms. It is important to remember that in his mature twelve-tone works Schoenberg did not think of the set in isolation, but always in context of the association of a given form with its IH-combinatorial counterpart. Thus Schoenberg sought out invariants that were preserved under the operations applied to *groups* of set forms and not just to individual sets. A good example of this can be seen in the choice of set forms for the recapitulation in the first movement of the Fourth String Quartet.

At the beginning of the movement P-o and I-5 with their retrogrades are the only set forms used. When P-o is stated together with I-5, five different tetrachords (by content) are formed when each of the six disjunct dyads of P-o is counterpointed against the dyads in equivalent order positions in I-5 (see Ex. 2.13). When the IH-combinatorial complex P-o/I-5 is transposed by a tritone, these tetrachords are held invariant, though reordered.[21]

In the Fourth String Quartet this property helps determine the choice for the transpositional level of the recapitulation.[22] The choice of T6 for the recapitulation is determined not through the characteristics

[21] This property is described and discussed in Andrew Mead, 'Large-Scale Strategy in Schoenberg's Twelve-Tone Music', *Perspectives of New Music*, 24 (1985), 126–7. He also mentions this property in 'Pedagogically Speaking: Manifestations of Pitch-Class Order', *In Theory Only*, 8 (1984), 28 n.

[22] Beyond the immediate relationships of this tetrachordal invariance, broader connections can be made between the exposition and the recapitulation because of the invariance of dyadic segments. For a discussion of this, see William Lake, 'Structural Functions of Segmental Interval-Class 1 Dyads in Schoenberg's Fourth Quartet, First Movement', *In Theory Only*, 8 (1984), 25.

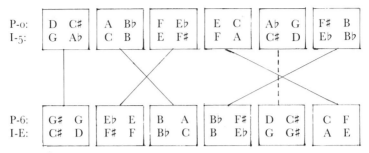

Ex. 2.13 Fourth String Quartet: tetrachords held invariant under T-6 of an
IH-combinatorial pair of set forms

of the set in isolation but through the properties of a given set form in
conjunction with its IH-combinatorial counterpart.

HEXACHORDAL LEVELS

In Schoenberg's mature twelve-tone music the normative subdivision
of the set is into hexachordal segments. Although other subdivisions do
occur, receiving local emphasis, in most of the mature works the hexachord is the fundamental unit of progression. The normative hexachordal subdivision of the set, taken together with the property of IH-
combinatoriality, has great significance for both local harmony and for
the large-scale formal organization of the work.

It is, of course, a feature of IH-combinatorial sets that the disjunct
hexachords are equivalent pitch-class sets. Because of this property, the
constant division of the set into hexachords in Schoenberg's mature
twelve-tone works is not merely a casual and convenient division, but
an active assertion and exploitation of the harmonic identity of the disjunct hexachords.[23]

The subdivision of the set into hexachords has significant consequences for the formal structure as well. Given an IH-combinatorial
set and local choice of set form characterized by membership in a given
IH-combinatorial complex, formal sections can be determined by the
content of the hexachords. For each such complex there are two, and
only two, hexachordal types (by content) and this pair of hexachords is
distinct from that of any other IH-combinatorial complex. For
example, in *Moses und Aron*, the first hexachords of P-o and RI-3, and
the second of I-3 and R-o all have the same pitch-class content: A Bb E
D D♯ C♯. None of the other 44 transformations have hexachords with
this content. Schoenberg exploited these hexachordal levels to characterize sections of form by the pitch-class content of the hexachords.

[23] See Babbitt, 'Set Structure', p.136.

It is well known that Schoenberg viewed the twelve-tone system as an answer to the many problems posed by the abandonment of tonality. A number of comments in his writings indicate his belief that twelve-tone music 'unleashed the potential of absolute music' and provided solutions not found in his earlier, atonal, compositions. One of the issues that had troubled him in those earlier works was form. He had noticed that his more extended atonal works were text settings and that he tended to articulate the formal structure not by internal pitch logic but, rather, by means of the differentiation provided for by the various sections of the text. From his statements it is evident that he was dissatisfied with the dependence of musical structure on an external feature.[24]

Schoenberg's concern with this problem was heightened by his awareness that in tonal music form was not an arbitrary motivic scheme, grafted on to the pitch language. In his discussion of form in tonal music Schoenberg remarked that the various sections of a tonal composition receive their identity, and the ability to be perceived as functionally separate, by the differentiation imparted by different key-centres.[25] Clearly, in his mature twelve-tone compositions Schoenberg felt he had found means of formal differentiation that originated in the pitch language and could substitute for the functions previously supplied by key centres in tonal music.[26] He accomplished this by the characterization of formal regions by hexachordal levels. Indeed, in a theoretical sense, there are some interesting correspondences between diatonic collections and hexachordal levels. For example, there are twelve diatonic collections each characterized by a particular pitch-class content distinct from any of the other diatonic collections. Similarly, for IH-combinatorial hexachords there are twelve hexachordal levels, each of which is determined by the pitch-class content of the disjunct hexachords.

In the mature twelve-tone works Schoenberg tends to treat the opening IH-combinatorial complex as a referential region, a kind of metaphor for the tonic in a tonal composition.[27] (Surely, though, it must be emphasized, there is no tonic, tonic chord, nor chordal functionality.)

---

[24] 'Composition with Twelve Tones (1)', *Style and Idea*, pp. 217–18.

[25] Ibid.

[26] Ibid., 218.

[27] As Babbitt remarked about the Concerto for Violin: 'For example, the four sets so associated [*an IH-combinatorial complex*] are the only sets employed during the first fifty-eight measures of the concerto and the area thus delineated is normatively closely analogous to a functional phonal area.' See his 'Three Essays', p. 49. Babbitt's assertion that these were the only sets used in the first fifty-eight measures of the composition was challenged by George Perle in 'Babbitt, Lewin, and Schoenberg: A Critique', *Perspectives of New Music*, 2 (1963), 120–7. In a response printed immediately following Perle's remarks Babbitt noted that the divergences from the combinatorial four-group were entirely local in character, a T4 cycle of transpositions. See 'Mr Babbitt Answers', ibid., 128–32.

Indeed, in most of Schoenberg's extended twelve-tone works from his mature period, he establishes at the beginning of the movement a region in which appear only those set forms from the initial, and thus referential, IH-combinatorial complex.

The establishment of a referential hexachordal level at the beginning of a movement became the linchpin of Schoenberg's large-scale formal design. Invariably the composition, having confirmed a privileged hierarchical status for this level by durational emphasis and temporal placement, then proceeds to other, secondary, hexachordal levels. The specific choice of those secondary levels is determined, not by any pre-ordained syntax, but rather by the structure of the set and the partitions employed.[28]

Characteristically, no secondary hexachordal region receives the durational stability and emphasis accorded the opening IH-combinatorial complex. Instead, these secondary areas are more or less transitory, providing local emphasis—perhaps comparable to a tonicization of a secondary scale degree in a tonal composition. The formal structure concludes with a return to the original referential hexachordal level, thus effecting an easily understood closure. The closing section, like its counterpart at the beginning of the composition, is emphasized by its temporal position and its comparative duration.

By such means Schoenberg created a logical twelve-tone equivalent for the differentiation previously supplied by key areas in tonal music, while at the same time providing a dynamic solution to the problem of form in non-tonal music. Of special significance is his ability to mould that form according to the specific structure of the set.

An important component of Schoenberg's treatment of hexachordal levels is his tendency to treat the hexachord as a harmonic unit. This is often accomplished by the repetition of the elements of the hexachord within a rhythmically defined span. In some of his mature compositions, most notably the Trio, Op.45, the tendency to consider the hexachord as the fundamental unit of progression led Schoenberg to use several different sets that produce multiple orderings of the source hexachords.

HARMONY

Schoenberg's twelve-tone harmony has provoked a good deal of controversy. Some of the earliest critics of his method claimed that Schoenberg had little rational control over this dimension. Doubts were expressed about his claim that the set could control all dimensions of

[28] See David Lewin, 'A Study of Hexachord Levels in Schoenberg's Violin Fantasy', *Perspectives of New Music*, 6 (1968), 18–32.

the fabric including the harmony.[29] According to this view, the harmonies on the surface of Schoenberg's twelve-tone music were arbitrary, lacking an organic relationship to the presumably referential set. Although the harmonic organization of the earliest twelve-tone works may warrant some criticism, in his mature twelve-tone works there is the most refined control over this dimension. In those compositions he dealt with this issue squarely and effectively, in a manner consistent with and derived from the properties of the referential set.

The clearest relationship between local harmony and the referential set is effected by creating linear or vertical structures from segments of the set. This kind of harmonic relationship is both obvious and simple, with a one-to-one relationship between local harmony and the structure of the set. This encourages an often-used technique whereby different set forms are related to one another by 'nestings' of equivalent segments.[30]

Similarly, Schoenberg exploited the association of non-adjacent elements of the set to create local harmonies that are equivalent to segments of the set.[31] Ex. 2.5, analysed above in the section on partitioning, is a good example of this kind of harmonic organization.[32]

---

[29] A good summary of the arguments about the extent to which the twelve-tone set can control twelve-tone harmony can be found in Hyde, *Schoenberg's Twelve-Tone Harmony*, pp. 18–23. A thorough survey of the pertinent literature is presented in pp. 153–4 n. 50.

[30] The concepts of nesting and segmental invariance between set forms are discussed by Lewin, 'A Theory of Segmental Association'. Lewin shows how such invariant segments are used by Schoenberg to foster both local and long-range associations between set forms.

[31] Babbitt refers to this as 'associative harmony in the small' and notes that it is employed in Schoenberg's twelve-tone works much as it had been in the earlier periods. See his 'Set Structure', p. 143.

[32] Hyde has argued that Schoenberg systematically exploits the harmonies embedded in the set in several dimensions. She further claims that Schoenberg's twelve-tone harmony, seen in this light, has a profound influence on set choice, phrasing, metre, and form. See the following: 'The Telltale Sketches: Harmonic Structure in Schoenberg's Twelve-Tone Method', *Musical Quarterly*, 66 (1980), 560–80; 'The Roots of Form in Schoenberg's Sketches', *Journal of Music Theory*, 24 (1980), 1–36; *Schoenberg's Twelve-Tone Harmony;* 'The Format and Function of Schoenberg's Twelve-Tone Sketches', *Journal of the American Musicological Society*, 36 (1983), 453–80; 'A Theory of Twelve-Tone Meter', *Music Theory Spectrum*, 6 (1984), 14–51; 'Musical Form and the Development of Schoenberg's Twelve-Tone Method', *Journal of Music Theory*, 29 (1985), 85–143. Although I find many of Hyde's analytical observations to be perceptive, I find myself in strong disagreement about her overall conclusions, particularly with regard to the role local twelve-tone harmonies play in the determination of set choice, the formation of metre, and the creation of form. A thorough critique of her claims would demand inordinate space and would be inappropriate here. Let me merely remark in this context that the recognition that Schoenberg's 'associative harmonies' play a central role in local relationships is an observation that stems from Babbitt and Perle, and is readily observable in all of Schoenberg's serial compositions. However, Hyde's extension of these ideas to an all-encompassing theory of Schoenberg's harmonic organization is faulty in at least two important respects. First, by attempting to account for all of Schoenberg's twelve-tone music, from Opp. 25–50, Hyde does not take into account the enormous changes that took place in Schoenberg's twelve-tone method during this period. Significantly, most of her analyses are from the earliest compositions: Opp. 23–9. The changes that took place during this period, and described in the present book, had an enormous impact on Schoenberg's harmonic

None the less, these relationships, however crucial for an understanding of Schoenberg's twelve-tone harmony, do not adequately account for significant aspects of harmonic structure in Schoenberg's mature style and therefore cannot be regarded as the sole determinant of harmony in those works.

It must be remembered that Schoenberg, in his later works, did not conceive of the set in isolation, but rather in conjunction with its IH-combinatorially related counterpart. This is sometimes explicitly apparent in his sketches, where it is clear that he was often accustomed to working out the ordering of the set at the same time as he was planning its combination with an IH-combinatorially related form.

This pervasive consistency of set combination thus has tremendous implications for harmonic structure, for the intervallic relationships formed between a given set form and its IH-combinatorial partner are an integral part of the harmonic vocabulary of Schoenberg's mature twelve-tone works. This is not to imply that there is a fixed sequence of dyads formed by notes of equivalent order position. Rather, the basis of Schoenberg's mature twelve-tone harmony lies in the hexachordal division of the set, its IH-combinatorial structure, and the opposition of order corresponding hexachords of IH-combinatorially related set forms.[33] In this way the structure of the set becomes the critical determinant of harmonic relationships.

This is so because the intervals most common within the hexachord are those most infrequent between the hexachords (and vice versa). This in turn allowed Schoenberg to create functional differentiation by the intervallic association of IH-combinatorially related set forms. This method of set combination was most intimately suited to Schoenberg's melody and accompaniment treatment. As an example, consider the interval-class content of the set of *Moses und Aron*. The hexachords of this set are both pitch-class set 012367 and thus their interval vector is $\{4, 2, 2, 2, 3, 2\}$. These fifteen interval classes represent the totality of interval classes found within each of the disjunct hexachords. At the same time the component interval classes of the disjunct hexachords are found in inverse multiplicity between those hexachords. In the present instance, the thirty-six interval classes found between the hexachord of this set and its complement can be described by the 'difference vector'

vocabulary. In particular we see Schoenberg moving from harmonic relationships dominated almost exclusively by local, associative harmony, to a more consistent and coherent 'combinatorial harmony'. Second, it is easily demonstrated that the surface of Schoenberg's twelve-tone compositions is covered with harmonies that are in no way equivalent to embedded harmonies of the set, even if one extends those harmonies (as Hyde does) to include 'around the corner' harmonies (e.g. a tetrachord with order positions t, e, o, 1). Hyde tends to deal with this issue by marking for attention only those pitch-class sets that are in fact equivalent to embedded harmonies of the set.

[33] This aspect of Schoenberg's twelve-tone harmonic vocabulary is briefly described by Babbitt in 'Set Structure', p. 136 and also in 'Three Essays', p. 50.

{4,8,8,8,6,2}. Those interval classes that occur least frequently within the hexachords occur most frequently between the hexachords and vice versa.[34] Therefore the structure of the set, and in particular the source hexachord, becomes the critical determinant of harmonic relationships in the mature twelve-tone compositions: the character of the intervallic relationships between hexachords is determined by the intervallic structure of the set.[35]

We have seen earlier that in the mature twelve-tone works—and this is in marked contrast to the early serial compositions—Schoenberg is extraordinarily consistent about set-form combinations. He states simultaneously only those forms that are IH-combinatorially related and does so exclusively by the association of order corresponding hexachords of I-related forms. This has important ramifications for the harmonic structure. By combining sets only in this way Schoenberg ensures that throughout the work there will be one, and only one, all-encompassing harmonic profile, and its properties are determined by the structure of the set.

Of course, the intervallic relationships between the first hexachords of IH-combinatorially related forms are identical to those formed between the second hexachords as well. Moreover, this very same harmonic profile also characterizes the relationships between the first and second hexachords of the set. This is of particular significance because of the compositionally normative hexachordal division of the set. Therefore, even without polyphonic combination of different set forms, the same combinatorial harmony results within the set because of the hexachordal division. Since Schoenberg generally creates areas comprised of combinatorially related set forms and subdivides the set into hexachords, it follows that this harmonic profile—his combinatorial harmony—characterizes all sections of the composition. It is the common denominator, a harmonic relationship that is a fixed constant, determined by the structure of the set and the norms of set combination and division (see Ex. 2.14).

In mm. 187–91 of Act I of *Moses und Aron* there is a passage in which the third cello and clarinets (marked with *Haupt-* and *Nebenstimme* respectively) present P-7 (mm. 187–8) and RI-t (mm. 189–91). At the same time the other voices present I-t and R-7, the normative kind of combination of set forms with their IH-combinatorially related counterparts.

The articulation of the surface effects a categorization into component hexachords. Within each measure the *Haupt-* and *Nebenstimme* are placed in opposition to the remaining parts. Thus, within each measure, those component elements of texture form a fixed class of in-

---

[34] Id., 'Set Structure', p.136.
[35] This point was made by Babbitt in 'Three Essays', p.50.

Ex. 2.14 *Moses und Aron*: combinatorial harmony
mm. 187–91

The combinatorial harmony determined by this set: difference vector 4, 8, 8, 8, 6, 2 occurs in this example:

1st hex. of P-7 and 1st hex. of I-t, m. 187
2nd hex. of P-7 and 2nd hex. of I-t, m. 188
1st hex. of P-7 and 2nd hex. of P-7, mm. 187–8
1st hex. of I-t and 2nd hex. of I-t, mm. 187–8
1st hex. of RI-t and 1st hex. of R-7, m. 189
2nd hex. of RI-t and 2nd hex. of R-7, mm. 190–1
1st hex. of RI-t and 2nd hex. of RI-t, mm. 189–91
1st hex. of R-7 and 2nd hex. of R-7, mm. 189–91

terval relationships, one determined by the structure of the set. At the same time, within each of these opposing elements of the texture, the selfsame intervallic relationships arise between the successive hexachords, a relationship that is underlined and emphasized by the sequential rhythmic design.

Thus, from this example it should be clear that this class of intervallic relationships, *combinatorial harmony*, saturates the compositional surface. Moreover, since the hexachordal subdivision of the set is normative, and since set combination is limited virtually exclusively to IH-combinatorially related set forms, it follows that this specific combinatorial harmony pervades the composition. Here we have a unifying, cohesive bond, one created by and peculiar to the structure of the referential set.

METRE

Metre in Schoenberg's mature twelve-tone compositions is related to his handling of the set and is neither a notational anachronism nor an arbitrary rhythmic device superimposed on the pitch structure.

In any music in which it is treated as a component element of temporal organization, metre can be created by a variety of non-pitch-relational features: the placement of dynamics, density, the durations of and between notes, and so forth. However, in tonal music such features are secondary in both power and subtlety to the pitch-relational means used to create metre, and, therefore, are rarely used in isolation. Rather, they serve to support and clarify pitch-derived metre.

Similarly, in twelve-tone music metre can be established solely by non-pitch parameters. However, excessive reliance on such parameters to form metre can create a crude, one-dimensional compositional surface. It is a mark of the scope of Schoenberg's stylistic development that he learned how to exploit pitch-relational characteristics in his compositions to form the metre, thus creating a subtle interaction between pitch and rhythm. He accomplished this primarily by exploiting the periodicity of pitch structures: the hexachord and aggregate.[36]

In the mature style aggregates are not occasional constructs, but so saturate the surface that it is often possible to divide the temporal continuum into a succession of aggregate statements. Schoenberg uses the periodicity determined by aggregate succession as the principal basis of metric formation.[37]

---

[36] Hyde has a similar, though in some ways significantly different, view of Schoenberg's metric formation. In line with her theory of Schoenberg's harmony, she sees metre as determined by the periodicity of harmonies equivalent to segments of the twelve-tone set. See *Schoenberg's Twelve-Tone Harmony*, chap. 4. This chapter is reworked and slightly expanded in her article, 'A Theory of Twelve-Tone Meter'.

[37] Babbitt has demonstrated the role aggregate rhythm plays in Schoenberg's music. See his brief discussion of this in relation to the third movement of the Fourth String Quartet, 'Set Structure', pp. 142–3.

Ex. 2.15 Fourth String Quartet, mm. 312–15: hexachordally determined metre

The division of the time line by the aggregate is by far the most prevalent basis for metric formation in the mature compositions. One can find hundreds of such examples, and indeed, a number of the examples cited earlier in this chapter clearly demonstrate this property (see Exs. 2.2, 2.3, 2.9, 2.14).

However, in addition, Schoenberg also uses the normative subdivision of the set into hexachords to establish the metre (see Ex. 2.15). Each hexachord in this example lasts a span of time equivalent to the written measure. Since the disjunct hexachords of IH-combinatorial sets are harmonically equivalent, this metre is founded not on the numerical equivalence of the segments but, rather, on their harmonic identity. This harmonic pitch-relational basis for the metre is supported by the durations, instrumentation, and so forth.

Aggregate and hexachord rhythm are not always neatly aligned with the written metre. Sometimes, when the harmonic rhythm is faster, the aggregate or hexachord is used to define beats and the metre is built up from these units. Or, if the harmonic rhythm is slower, an aggregate might unfold over several measures.

Moreover, in many of Schoenberg's compositions there are no, or almost no, changes in the notated metre. (A good example is the first movement of the Fourth String Quartet). This does not mean, however, that there are no changes in the actual metre. Rather, Schoenberg seems to have preferred not to indicate every local deviation from the written metre, both for practical reasons and because in these works the written metre was treated as referential—a metric standard somewhat analogous in compositional function to the referential hexachordal level. A good illustration of the use of this technique can be seen in mm. 24–31 of the Fourth String Quartet (see Ex. 2.16).

In the first five measures of this excerpt there is a strikingly clear correlation between aggregate, or pairs of aggregates, and metre. The result is a four-square expression of the referential metric. But, in mm. 29–31 this regularity is broken and the metre is displaced to the middle of the written measure. This metric displacement is in the service of the larger compositional design. The opening referential combinatorial complex, CC-0, provides the totality of set forms used in mm. 1–31 of the composition. Starting at the end of m. 31 Schoenberg begins to exploit other hexachordal levels. The clear aggregate-derived formation and emphasis of the referential metre in mm. 24—8 and then the dissolution of that regularity work hand in hand with the move to a new hexachordal level. The transition to a new hexachordal level (CC-5) is paralleled and therefore emphasized by the concurrent metric shift.[38]

MULTIDIMENSIONAL SET PRESENTATIONS

Earlier, in the discussion of aggregates, several examples were presented in which middleground aggregates resulted from the conjunction of elements from a number of local set forms. Instances of this procedure are quite common in Schoenberg's mature twelve-tone music. By these means Schoenberg created a multidimensional compositional surface in which both local and long-range events relate back to a common referential origin.

Starting in 1926 Schoenberg also learned how to form a specialized kind of middleground structure in which a linear presentation of the set unfolds slowly in one line or part, the product of extracting elements from up to twelve local set forms.

Some of the most interesting examples of multidimensional set presentations occur in the Variations for Orchestra, Op.31. Starting in m. 34, after the introduction, P-0, and the three other members of its IH-combinatorial complex (RI-9, R-0, I-9) are stated in succession as a line in the cello. This thematic presentation of the set forms that make up CC-0 becomes the basis of each of the nine variations as well as the Finale.

In the fifth Variation the theme appears in the lowermost register, unfolding slowly over the course of the variation (see Ex. 2.17). This is

---

[38] Hyde makes a similar point about Schoenberg's tendency to initiate sections with a clearly defined metre, and then counter that clarity in the course of the development. See 'A Theory of Twelve-Tone Meter', p.50.

Ex. 2.16 Fourth String Quartet, mm. 24–31: aggregate and metre

Ex. 2.17 Variations for Orchestra, mm. 178–80: multidimensional set pre-
sentation

not a foreground presentation of this set but, rather, a middleground
thematic statement. Here is a true twelve-tone hierarchy with both the
slowly unfolding theme and its supportive local set forms derived from
the same referential idea. The slowly unfolding theme in the lowest
register is not a random concatenation of elements from local set forms
but, rather, results from the conjunction of like order positions from a
succession of isomorphically partitioned set forms.[39]

The use of isomorphic partitioning, in conjunction with the uniform
assignment of durations, guarantees a periodic harmonic structure.
The consistent placement of order positions with respect to the beat ensures that any given point in a beat will be harmonically equivalent to
that same point in any other beat within a segment. Thus, for example,
the harmony formed by the trumpet and first and second trombones in
the first beat of m. 178 is pitch-class set 012345 and is equivalent to the
pitch-class set at the corresponding points in the second and third beats
of this measure as well as the first and second beats of the following
measure.

In the initial presentation of the theme in m. 34 the first set statement
was subdivided into segments of five, four, and three elements. The fifth
variation replicates that subdivision: orchestrational contrast marks off
the segments of the theme. Moreover, each of the segments is characterized by its own partitioning. Thus, the five local set forms of the first
segment of the theme are isomorphically partitioned and this partitioning is distinct from that of the following two segments.

The regular alternation of P- and I-forms seen in this example is a
necessary component of this method of multidimensional set presentation, for that alternation ensures the hierarchical supremacy of the
slowly evolving theme. A succession limited to prime or inversional
forms would have produced parallel statements of the theme in the
other voices. Because of the regular alternation of P- and I-forms this
cannot occur.

It also follows that given isomorphic partitioning, consistent choice
of one order position for the evolving principal line, the alternation of
P- and I-forms, and an initial choice for the first set form, the remaining transformations are predetermined. For example, with B♭ as the
first note of the theme, there are four possibilities for the first local set
form, and of these Schoenberg chooses I-o. After this, given that the

[39] There is an interesting sketch-page in which Schoenberg works out the multidimensional
structure. At the bottom of the page Schoenberg wrote a note indicating some of the troubles he
had in recalling this idea after an interruption. Schoenberg's remarks are printed in Rufer, *The
Works of Arnold Schoenberg*, trans. Dika Newlin (London, 1962), 53. A facsimile of this sketch-page,
as well as a brief discussion of this passage, appear in Hyde, 'The Format and Function', pp.466–
7. Dahlhaus suggests that this sketch-page refers to the sixth variation. See his *Arnold Schönberg Variationen für Orchester, op. 31* (Munich: 1968), p. 24. However, the sets used make it certain that this
sketch refers to the fifth variation.

next note of the theme is E and that this must be order position o from a prime form, then the only choice for that form is P-6.

This mastery of twelve-tone technique—the construction of both local and long-range events from the same referential material and the interaction of partitioning and rhythm—represents a crucial dividing line in Schoenberg's stylistic growth as a twelve-tone composer. By Op.31 the set had become a referential idea, not merely for local melodic figures, but for the harmony, the form, the metre, as well as, in specialized situations, middleground melodic control.

In the preceding discussion, ten features characteristic of Schoenberg's mature twelve-tone style have been isolated and described. These features appear in, and sometimes saturate, the twelve-tone works from Op.32. However, it would be an error to conclude that these were ten separate traits related only by their common occurrence in a group of compositions. To the contrary, one of the supreme achievements of Schoenberg's mature twelve-tone style is the interdependence and interaction of the various dimensions.

A thorough understanding of how these features relate to and are dependent on one another can best be gained by retracing Schoenberg's steps from the beginning of the formation of the serial idea up through those pieces in which he reached full maturity in his handling of the system. We will then be able to see how each characteristic was introduced as part of a developing critical process that sought to make the structure of the set the compositional determinant for all dimensions of the musical fabric.

3

Before the Beginning
Die Jakobsleiter *and Other Incomplete Compositions, 1914–1918*

ALTHOUGH his first complete serial compositions were written in 1920, the real beginnings of Schoenberg's new method can be traced back to 1914. Schoenberg himself outlined some of the principal steps in the development of the idea:

The first step happened about December 1914 or at the beginning of 1915 when I sketched a symphony, the last part of which became later the 'Jakobsleiter,' but which never has been continued. The Scherzo of this symphony was based on a theme consisting of the twelve tones. But this was only one of the themes.[1]

Similarly, around 1948, in a short article about his twelve-tone music, Schoenberg recalled the way he had arrived at his method:

Ever since 1906–8, when I had started writing compositions which led to the abandonment of tonality, I had been busy finding methods to replace the structural functions of harmony. Nevertheless, my first distinct step toward this goal occurred only in 1915. I had made plans for a great symphony of which *Die Jakobsleiter* should be the last movement. I had sketched many themes, among them one for a scherzo which consisted of all the twelve tones. An historian will probably some day find in the exchange of letters between Webern and me how enthusiastic we were about this.

My next step in this direction—in the meantime I had been in the Austrian Army—occurred in 1917, when I started to compose *Die Jakobsleiter*. I had contrived the plan to provide for unity—which was always my main motive: to build all the main themes of the whole oratorio from a row of six tones—C-sharp, D, E, F, G, A-flat.[2]

Schoenberg's recollection of the principal stages in the development of the serial idea is confirmed by his manuscripts and sketches. The Scherzo fragment of 1914–15 does indeed represent the earliest layers of serial and twelve-tone thinking. Moreover, the compositional organization of the *Jakobsleiter* fragment conforms very closely to Schoen-

---

[1] The quote is from a letter to Slonimsky. See Nicolas Slonimsky, *Music Since 1900* (4th edn., New York, 1971), 1315. Schoenberg's recollection of the dating is probably faulty. The manuscript of the first fragment from the Scherzo has the date 27 May 1914.

[2] 'Composition with Twelve Tones, (2)', in *Style and Idea*, ed. Leonard Stein, trans. Leo Black (New York, 1975), 247.

berg's description and constitutes another important stage in his stylistic development. However, in addition, Schoenberg worked on several other fragments during this period. The compositional experience gained in these incomplete works played an important role in preparing Schoenberg for his serial revolution.

Had the proposed symphony of 1914–15 been completed, it would have dwarfed any previous symphony—both in length and in the enormous resources necessary to perform it. Preserved in the Schoenberg archives is a page on which Schoenberg sketched out the formal plan for this work. It shows that at one point he was planning a two-part symphony; the first part alone would have consisted of three movements.[3] The second movement was to have been a large scherzo. On another sketch-sheet Schoenberg outlined the major formal divisions of that movement:

2. Satz: (Scherzo) Die Lebenslust I Teil Scherzo mit 2 Trios, II Teil Reprise des ganzen mit Gesang.

   a) Dehmel Schöne wilde Welt Seite   10: Freudenruf
   b)   ,,   ,,   ,,   ,,   ,,   70: Götterhochzeit
   c)   ,,   ,,   ,,   ,,   ,,   117: Aeonische Stunde

In 1914 Schoenberg worked out a little over 100 measures of the Scherzo before putting it aside. He also sketched bits and pieces of the remainder of the movement, including some of the vocal sections. The following year (1915) he came back to this composition, sketched a new version of the beginning, but then stopped work, this time never to return.

These documents—the drafts of 1914 and 1915 together with their associated sketches—represent the earliest layers of Schoenberg's twelve-tone thinking, and give us an opportunity to examine his first experiments with serial organization. It is here that we can trace some of the critical stages in Schoenberg's compositional thinking on the eve of his revolution.

The draft of 1914 spans 103 measures, setting forth the principal lines of continuity. Although some passages are fully worked out, for others Schoenberg wrote down only the principal voice. Moreover, in addition to this continuity draft, many sketches have survived, including ones in which Schoenberg worked out individual passages before entering them into the continuity draft, as well as a number of isolated ideas, evidently intended for the second half of the movement.[4]

---

[3] A description of the plan for the symphony, with a persuasive interpretation of the numbering of the movements listed in this sketch is given in Walter Bailey, *Programmatic Elements in the Works of Arnold Schoenberg* (Ann Arbor, 1984), 84–103.

[4] Bailey gives a good account of the role of each of the sketches and their place in the scheme of the movement, ibid., 103–18.

The Scherzo begins with a repeating twelve-tone theme, stated in the clarinets (see Ex. 3.1).

The very presence of all twelve tones—each stated once and only once—is what endows this theme with such critical historical importance. Here Schoenberg takes the first conscious step towards the twelve-tone idea. Of course, for some time the informal circulation of all twelve pitch classes had been a recurrent feature of Schoenberg's compositions. But the Scherzo theme was something significantly, and most self-consciously, different.

In contrast to the procedures in Schoenberg's earlier contextual compositions, this theme is carefully formulated to include each pitch class once, and only once. Moreover, the theme is emphasized by its placement: it occurs at the very beginning of the work and is clearly meant to be the principal theme of the movement.

There is no question but that this theme had great significance for Schoenberg. In later years not only did he quite clearly and accurately remember its existence, but he also recognized that it marked the beginning of his twelve-tone odyssey. Moreover, in 1914 he was so excited about this new idea he could not keep it to himself. He disclosed the existence of this theme to Webern, who, stimulated by his mentor's excitement, adopted the idea. This occasioned no small amount of resentment and jealousy on the part of Schoenberg who felt betrayed by what he saw as the theft of his great idea.[5]

However significant the twelve-tone theme may be for the history of

---

[5] See Joan Smith, *Schoenberg and His Circle: A Viennese Portrait* (New York, 1986), 184–7. At first, it seems as if Schoenberg was happy to discuss this new idea with Webern. It will be recalled that in 'Composition with Twelve Tones (1)' Schoenberg remarked of his symphony that 'I had sketched many themes, among them one for a scherzo which consisted of all the twelve tones. An historian will probably some day find in the exchange of letters between Webern and me how enthusiastic we were about this' (p.247). But that enthusiasm and camaraderie waned. In 1951, old and embittered, jealous of the attention Webern was getting as the originator of ideas he considered his own, Schoenberg directed a blast at Webern. Upon hearing that Webern had claimed to be the inventor of *Klangfarbenmelodien* Schoenberg angrily retorted: 'Anyone who knows me at all knows that this is not true. It is known that I should not have hesitated to name Webern, had his music stimulated me to invent this expression. One thing is certain: even had it been Webern's idea, he would not have told it to me. He kept secret everything "new" he had tried in his compositions. I, on the other hand, immediately and exhaustively explained to him each of my new ideas (with the exception of the method of composition with twelve tones—that I long kept secret, because, as I said to Erwin Stein, Webern immediately uses everything I do, plan or say, so that— I remember my words—"By now I haven't the slightest idea who I am.")', 'Anton Webern: *Klangfarbenmelodie*', in *Style and Idea*, p.484. Apparently after his experience with the Scherzo, Schoenberg did not readily confide his compositional secrets to Webern. A hint of this loss of confidence is unwittingly cited by Webern. In his series of lectures entitled 'The Path to Twelve-note Composition', Webern remarked, 'But already in the spring of 1917—Schoenberg lived in the Gloriettegasse at the time, and I lived quite near—I went to see him one fine morning, to tell him I had read in some newspaper where a few groceries were to be had. In fact I disturbed him with this, and he explained to me that he was "on the way to something quite new." He didn't tell me more at the time, and I racked my brains—"For goodness' sake, whatever can it be?"', Anton Webern, *The Path to the New Music*, trans. Leo Black (Bryn Mawr, 1963), 44.

Ex. 3.1 The opening of the Scherzo from the proposed symphony of 1914–15;
the twelve-tone theme

Schoenberg's idea, very little in the structure of the Scherzo even remotely resembles the twelve-tone technique of later years. That this is the earliest layer of serial and twelve-tone thinking is borne out by the rudimentary serial procedures in this fragment.[6]

The very limited presence of the twelve-tone theme itself is a clear indication that Schoenberg was not thinking of that theme as the referential serial basis of the composition. Indeed, over the course of the 103 measures of the sketch, the complete twelve-tone theme only appears a few times: mm. 1–5, 12–16, 23–26.

Even more telling than the minimal exposure given to the twelve-tone theme is the exceptionally limited view of the operation of transposition. Although the twelve-tone theme appears at two transpositional levels, each time it is in precisely the same registral, durational, metric, and intervallic form—i.e., there is no particular reason to call these *serial* transformations. Nothing would distinguish the use of the operation of transposition in this context from the use of transposition in any prior age.

Yet, at the same time that the twelve-tone theme is limited to a few, isolated places, and even while the transpositions of the theme seem to show a completely traditional view of those operations, other aspects of the musical organization of this fragment reveal Schoenberg taking

[6] In spite of its importance as one of the first steps in the development of the twelve-tone idea, the Scherzo has received virtually no analytical attention. The only article is Fusako Hamao, 'On the Origin of the Twelve-Tone Method: Schoenberg's Sketches for the Unfinished *Symphony* (1914–1915)', *Current Musicology* 42 (1986), 32–45.

perceptible strides towards the development of the twelve-tone serial idea.

In the first measures, the twelve-tone theme is stated twice, without alteration, while beneath it the trumpets give a punctuated accompaniment of three trichords (see Ex. 3.1). In later years such an accompaniment would be formed by partitioning one of the transformations of the set into its discrete trichords and placing the resultant chords in the accompaniment. That is not the case here. Clearly, at this early stage, Schoenberg had not yet developed the notion that the intervallic order of the theme could, or should, be the exclusive, referential source of all musical events.

However, although these chords are not formed from a partitioned set form, they do relate back to the twelve-tone theme, and in a manner that emphasizes the conceptual links between Schoenberg's earlier contextual compositions and the serial compositions to come.

Within any twelve-tone set there are ten embedded trichords (order-positions 012, 123, 234 . . .9te). For this theme, no fewer than five of the trichords are pitch-class set 016—half of the possible embeddings.

Schoenberg exploits this property to form his accompaniment. The preponderance of pitch-class set 016 within the theme is mirrored by the chordal punctuation in the trumpets: both the second and third of those trichords are pitch-class set 016.

Throughout Schoenberg's contextual period this kind of association of linear and chordal events was hardly an unusual feature. However, here, although the systematic connections with past practice are most evident, we can see the beginnings of a fundamental conceptual change. In this case, and in other instances to come, the associations relate back to a single, referential, linear idea—the twelve-tone theme—and are not simply part of a continuously developing, varied succession of such associations. Thus, the twelve-tone theme, stated as a line at the beginning of the composition, is the principal referential source for subsequent events, both linear and chordal. This referential primacy clearly differentiates this fragment from Schoenberg's past practice.[7] It points the way to the future, where the imposed ordering of the chromatic would become the referential source for all surface events.

Further signs of this nascent conceptual change are visible in the continuation. The theme and its accompaniment of mm. 1–3 are repeated in mm. 3–5 and then followed by a transitional passage. This begins with a third statement of the theme but before it is completed the line

---

[7] Concerning his pre-First World War works Schoenberg remarked: 'Intoxicated by the enthusiasm of having freed music from the shackles of tonality, I had thought to find further liberty of expression. In fact, I myself and my pupils Anton von Webern and Alban Berg, and even Alois Hába believed that now music could renounce motivic features and remain coherent and comprehensible nevertheless.' See 'My Evolution', *Style and Idea*, p.88.

Ex. 3.2 The transitional six-note theme (mm. 8–11). This is a variant of a segment of the principal twelve-tone theme

changes direction, moving, in mm. 8–11, to a six-note theme, stated four times (see Ex. 3.2).

This new theme, like the chordal accompaniment of mm. 1–4, is not a segment of the twelve-tone theme. However, as was the case with those chords, this hexachord is derived from that theme. Not only is the opening dyad of this six-note motive held fixed in register but five of its six notes are a reordering of a segment of the twelve-tone theme: more evidence that the twelve-tone theme is not just one theme among many, but the principal source idea.

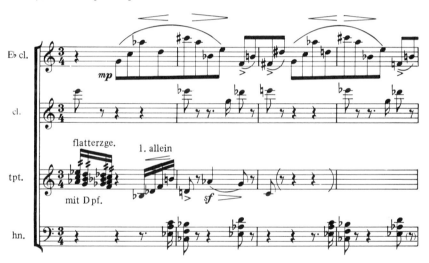

Ex. 3.3 mm. 12–15 of the Scherzo

In m. 12 the twelve-tone theme reappears, but this time in transposition.[8] In mm. 12–22 Schoenberg transposes mm. 1–11 (T = 5). The only changes are the addition of two voices in the accompaniment. But, once again, although these new voices are not set statements, they do relate back to the twelve-tone theme (see Ex. 3.3). The two successive

[8] Surely it cannot have escaped Schoenberg's attention that the transposition of a twelve-tone theme also contains all twelve tones. Of course, as Milton Babbitt has pointed out, a central difference between the twelve-tone system and the musical systems that preceded it is the difference between a permutational and a combinational system. See 'Twelve-tone Invariants as Compositional Determinants', *Musical Quarterly*, 46 (1960), 247–8.

tetrachords of the trumpet line in mm. 12–14 are both equivalent to pitch-class sets embedded within the twelve-tone theme. The first tetrachord (B♭ D♭ F B), pitch-class set 0137, is equivalent to the final tetrachord of the twelve-tone theme, while the next four notes (D A♭ G C) form pitch-class set 0157, equivalent to the first tetrachord.[9]

From mm. 23–31 Schoenberg proceeds to a statement of the material of mm. 1–11 and 12–22 at a new transpositional level. As before, he transposes the entire complex and, again, adds more voices: starting in m. 25 he adds P-0 with its accompaniment in parallel motion to P-7, and in mm. 27–8, P-5 as well.

The next passage, mm. 32–5 is of special significance (see Ex. 3.4).

Ex. 3.4 mm. 32–5 of the Scherzo: the eight-note theme in canon with accompaniment

(This is a conflation of the version in the draft and the corresponding sketch. Schoenberg noted on his draft 'Siehe 3a' indicating the chords from the sketch that he apparently did not want to copy on to the draft.

[9] Hamao asserts that the four-note figure in the clarinet (E, E♭, G, D♭) is derived from the discrete trichords of the set (see 'On the Origin,' pp.40–1). On a sketch-page Schoenberg did write out the four discrete trichords of the theme and it is also the case that the top line of these trichords contains the four pitch classes of this motive. (On the sketch-page this is worked out for P-0. With the appropriate transpositions it could be adapted to P-5.) That may indeed be the origin of this

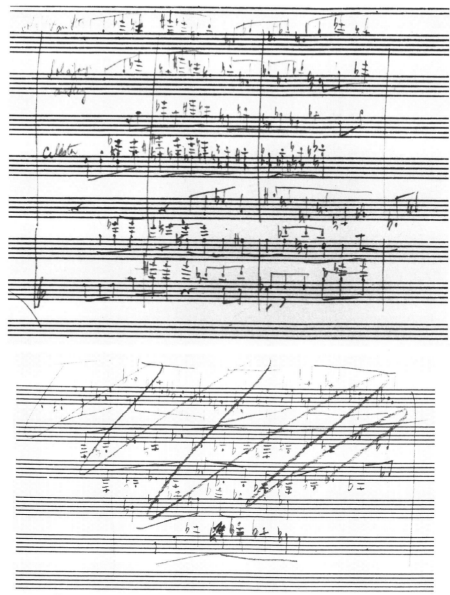

Ex. 3.5 Two earlier versions of the canonic imitation of Ex. 3.4

motive. However, the four trichords do not appear anywhere in the surviving compositional fragment. It is possible that Schoenberg intended to enter them somewhere—this is, after all, only a
sketch, not a fully worked out version—but it is difficult to see where such trichords would have
gone. However, without the trichords, the derivation of the melody from the trichords makes little
sense: it is missing the crucial intermediate step. That would be most unlike Schoenberg. Thus,
lacking a sketch with the trichords in a compositional context, the derivation of the clarinet
melody cannot be regarded as certain.

Schoenberg states an eight-note motive in canonic imitation, supported both by a countermelody and a chordal accompaniment. This passage seems to have given Schoenberg some trouble, for in the sketches are two prior, rejected versions of these measures (see Ex. 3.5).

In the first of these Schoenberg stated the original twelve-tone theme in canonic imitation. Each new voice entered at a time-interval of one eighth-note. In the process, Schoenberg came up with an interesting, if limiting, solution to the problem of the relationship between a linearly stated theme and the chords created by simultaneous statements of that theme. Because the successive entries are an eighth-note apart, each vertical represents a segment of the theme. Here is one of Schoenberg's first solutions to the problem of serial harmony.

The other rejected version of mm. 32–5 presents a similar canon, with the same resultant equivalence between horizontal and vertical structures. However, the theme used is not the twelve-tone theme: it contains only eight tones. An understanding of the origins of this eight-note theme sheds some interesting light on Schoenberg's understanding of the properties of serial organization at this early stage in his development of the idea.

On another sketch-sheet Schoenberg wrote out the twelve-tone theme. Directly beneath the theme he placed the inversion, I-0. Here, and in two other places on this sketch-sheet, Schoenberg marked order-positions 5–8 for attention. He did so because they are held invariant under retrograde inversion (see Ex. 3.6).

This invariant relationship prompted the structure of the eight-tone theme used in canonic imitation.[10] That theme is formed from the eight tones left over when the four invariant tones are removed. The first five notes of the twelve-tone theme are preserved in their original order while the last three are rearranged slightly. Here, for the first time, is concrete musical evidence of Schoenberg's exploitation of invariance in a serial context.

The final version of this passage—as it appears in mm. 32–5 and the associated sketch sheet—is based on this eight-note theme. However, that version (Ex. 3.4, above) diverges significantly from the earlier, rejected sketches.

Schoenberg changed the time-interval of imitation from one eighth to two. On the face of it, this might seem to be a retreat from the identification of the horizontal with the vertical that had characterized the earlier versions of this passage. After all, in the earlier sketches Schoenberg had created vertical harmonies identical to segments of the theme. But Schoenberg has seen another way to accomplish the same thing. Since all even-numbered order positions occur on the beat and all odd-

[10] This is pointed out by Hamao, 'On the Origin', p. 36–9.

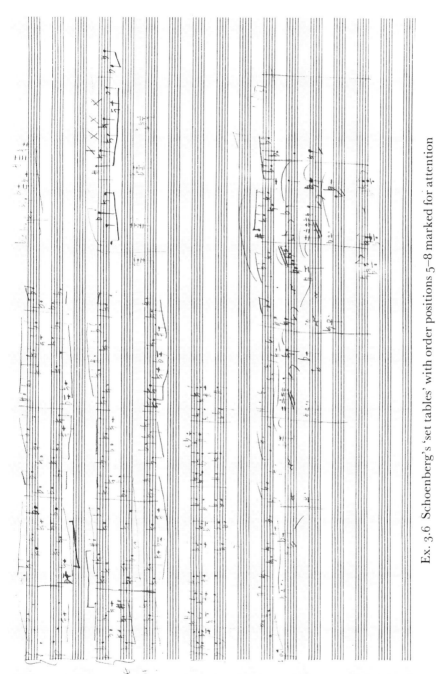

Ex. 3.6 Schoenberg's 'set tables' with order positions 5–8 marked for attention

numbered order positions fall off the beat, it follows that once four voices have entered there must be a regular alternation of two, and only two chords. (This is in contrast to the prior versions where each successive eighth brought into play a different vertical combination.) Significantly, these two chords (pitch-class sets 0137 and 0157) are equivalent to segments of the original twelve-tone theme: the first and last tetrachords. Of course, we have already seen a similar relationship: in mm. 12–13 the trumpets also presented tetrachords equivalent to the first and third tetrachords of the original theme.

In counterpoint to this canon Schoenberg added a line that included the pitch classes C B F E, i.e., the four pitch classes omitted from the eight-note theme. Thus, together with the eight-note theme, these four pitch classes complete the chromatic, yet another sign of Schoenberg's emerging twelve-tone thinking.

Ex. 3.7 An eight-note theme, derived from the tetrachords of mm. 32–40

The canon-derived chords continue until m. 40, and then Schoenberg closes off this section of the Scherzo with two statements of yet another eight-note theme (see Ex. 3.7). This theme was derived from the chords (mm. 32–5) that had resulted from the canon.[11] This is shown clearly by a sketch where Schoenberg works this out (see Ex. 3.8). Schoenberg arranged the eight notes of the two chords in ascend-

Ex. 3.8 The sketch for the melody in mm. 41–3

[11] This is pointed out ibid., p.43–4.

ing order starting from D. Over each note he wrote either a 'I' or a '2', depending on whether the note in question belonged to the first or the second of the two canon-derived chords. Then he composed the melody of Ex. 3.7, alternating between notes from the first and second tetrachords.

With the conclusion of this figure we have come to the end of the first section of the Scherzo. Starting in m. 44, Schoenberg begins a contrasting section which continues until m. 71 and contains no statements of the twelve-tone theme, nor any of the derived motives. Clearly, at this early stage in his development Schoenberg was not yet ready, or able, either to saturate the fabric with the set, or to include it in all of the sections of the piece. That universal presence would have to wait until Schoenberg had developed enough skill with serial techniques so that he would recognize it was possible to generate sufficient variety from a single referential ordering.

Starting in m. 72 reminiscences of the opening section recur with the reappearance of the alternating, canon-derived chords, the four-note countermelody from mm. 32 ff, and, finally, fragments of the beginning of the twelve-tone theme and its P-5 transposition. Included in this brief section is an interesting passage, one that gives more evidence of Schoenberg's emerging interest in serially derived invariants (see Ex. 3.9). In mm. 75–6 the flutes state the first five notes of P-0. At the same time order positions 5–8—the notes held invariant between P-0 and I-0—appear in the trumpet. Then, in mm. 77–8, Schoenberg states the first five notes of P-5 in the flutes while order positions 5–8 appear in the trumpet. In the process, an interesting property emerges.

Order positions 5–8 of P-0 are C B F E. The same order positions in P-5 are F E B♭ A; the last two notes of this segment in P-0 are the first two in P-5. Schoenberg exploits this invariance to create a new figure, a hexachord (mm. 76–8, trumpet), that is a conflation of order positions 5–8 from P-0 and P-5. Here, in its most rudimentary form, is one of the basic building-blocks of Schoenberg's twelve-tone technique.

Ex. 3.9 mm. 74–8 of the Scherzo

After some more contrasting material, and a few references to prior figures, we come to the close of the 103 measure continuity draft of 1914. However, in addition to this draft, there are a number of isolated sketches, some clearly intended for the second half of this movement—the reprise with voices. Although most of these sketches—like the corresponding sections from the continuity draft—are not serially organized, one sketch illustrates Schoenberg's gradually emerging recognition of the possibilities of serial organization (see Ex. 3.10). The final three measures of this sketch present the first few notes of a statement of P-0, followed, in close succession, by the beginnings of several transpositions. What is so important about these few measures is that the choice of transpositions is determined by the structure of the twelve-tone theme.

Ex. 3.10 A passage intended for the Scherzo

The first five pitches in the upper voice are the first five order positions of P-0. But this voice does not continue on with the next notes from the twelve-tone theme. Instead, the lower voice answers the top voice with the succession E A F B E C D♭. This can be understood in two ways—as an imitative statement of the theme, or, somewhat loosely, as continuing the statement of P-0 begun in the upper voice. That both of these interpretations of this passage were intended by Schoenberg is confirmed by a preparatory sketch (see Ex. 3.11).

In the first sketch in the example (a), Schoenberg states the twelve-tone theme partitioned between two voices. Then, immediately below (b), recognizing the similarity of the lower partitioned voice to a statement of a transposition, he starts a statement of P-2. The result is something that is both a transposition, and a continuation of the set of the upper line.

However, the importance of this passage is not limited to its exploitation of properties of the theme to determine the transpositions.

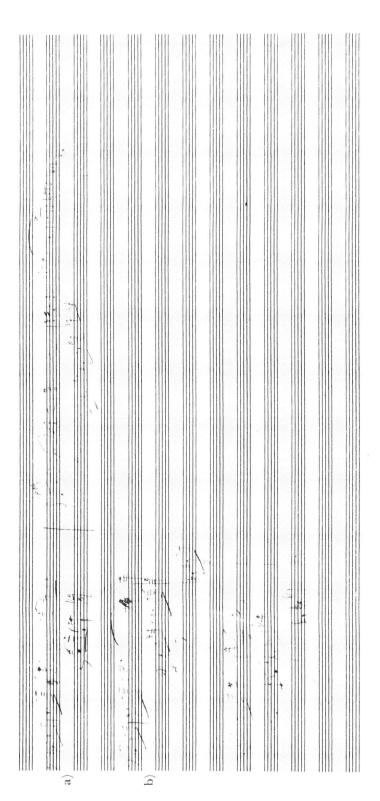

Ex. 3.11 A sketch for Ex. 3.10

Although the serial idea may have clear historical roots, it is no mere extension of the operations of transposition, inversion, and retrograde as they were understood in prior eras. There is a fundamental and absolutely crucial distinction between the serial operations of transposition, inversion, and retrogression and their historical antecedents. In the eighteenth century, a 'transposition' that did not preserve rhythm and contour would be unrecognizable as such. Truly serial operations, by contrast, have no such presupposition of preservation of rhythm, contour, or anything else except for interval order.[12]

Up to this point, all of the statements of the twelve-tone theme can be understood to conform to the historically determined idea of transposition. However, the partitioned statement of the theme, seen in this sketch, reveals a more abstract conception of that operation. Schoenberg's twelve-tone *theme* was on the verge of becoming a twelve-tone *set*.

Eventually, in later compositions, Schoenberg would be able to derive all events on the surface from a single referential ordering. (Unity, after all, was his 'main motive'.) To do this, however, he could not merely restate the set in one fixed motivic pattern, for—as he indicated above—he knew he would not be able to generate a sufficient variety of different themes and subsidiary material. Here, in this sketch, we see the first steps in the direction of an abstract conception of the twelve-tone set that would make such exhaustive accountability possible.

Other passages in the sketches confirm that Schoenberg was feeling his way to the serial idea. Most of these are on one sketch-page (refer back to Ex. 3.6).

In one of these sketches (staves 8–9) Schoenberg has taken the notes of P-o, I-o, R-o and RI-o, divided them into their discrete tetrachords, and stated them as chords.[13] Similarly, up and to the right on the same page (staves 4–6), Schoenberg sketched out another passage in which the twelve-tone theme was accompanied by its discrete trichords, rotated to avoid octave duplications. Neither of these sketches corresponds to any of the passages in the compositional sketches. Rather, these two passages are a further indication of Schoenberg's interest in manipulating the theme, varying it, rearranging its notes.

After some time—it is not exactly clear how long—Schoenberg interrupted his work on the Scherzo. He returned to it the following

---

[12] Moreover, there are 'profound differences between the twelve-tone system and those musical systems in which the "historical forerunners" of the twelve-tone operations appear. The crucial point here is that these "forerunners" are not independent and fundamental structural determinants, but means of immediate procedure, neither necessarily present nor, if present, of more than local significance and influence.' See Babbitt, 'Twelve-Tone Invariants', p.246.

[13] The statement of RI-4 contains two deviations from the referential ordering. It is possible that Schoenberg simply erred in writing out these set forms, but it is also possible that the deviation was intended for some reason. In any event, the deviations are preserved in the vertical tetrachords in the sketch.

year, starting a new draft on 4 May 1915. Schoenberg worked on this version for an undetermined period, wrote out five pages of draft and sketches, then put it aside, never to return.

Much of this fragment is merely a reworking of the draft of the previous year: some passages are taken over with few alterations; others are altered, though still recognizable. However, significantly, some of the newly composed passages reveal Schoenberg's continued interest in the serial idea.

The forty-seven measure fragment appears in the first five pages of Schoenberg's Fourth Sketch-book (p.1: mm. 1–5; p.2: mm. 6–28; p.5: mm. 29–47). Moreover, scattered among the pages are a number of sketches, some of which were incorporated into the fragment, others that were either rejected or never reached before Schoenberg broke off work.

Measures 1–5 present an imitatively stated ostinato, somewhat analogous to the opening of the 1914 draft. This theme is made up of the beginning nine notes of the twelve-tone theme of the previous year.

After varying the continuation in m. 5, Schoenberg introduces another familiar figure, the four-note motive, order positions 5–8 of the twelve-tone theme, the notes held invariant between P-0 and I-0 (see Ex. 3.12). Accompanying this figure are repeated chords made up of order positions 0–4.

Ex. 3.12 m. 6 of the 1915 draft

Earlier, it was emphasized that the concept of serial organization was dependent on the development of an abstract view of the material: a twelve-tone set is not merely a theme with fixed register, durations, and articulations. The passage in Ex. 3.12, with its chords derived from the first five order positions and its melody from the next four, offers tangible evidence of Schoenberg's continuing development of serial thinking. This is no mere literal restatement of the nine-note theme, but a serial elaboration.

On the same page in the sketch-book, and then on the next, are two other, very similar sketches (see Ex. 3.13). Through their mix of chord and melody as well as their alteration of the rhythm of the original theme, these isolated sketches testify to the gradual emergence of serial thinking. Starting at m. 15 Schoenberg moves to a contrasting section, virtually identical to the contrasting section of the previous year (mm. 15–29 of the 1915 version are equivalent to mm. 44–71 in the 1914 fragment). Schoenberg does not retain mm. 72–91 of the 1914 version but instead jumps directly to a statement of the passage that had been mm. 92–6 in 1914, extending it slightly (mm. 30–47 in the 1915 draft).

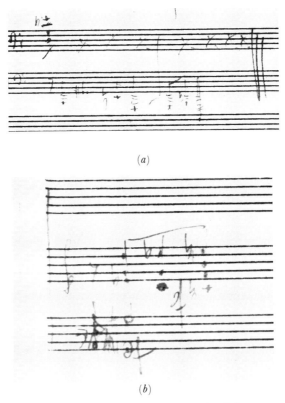

(a)

(b)

Ex. 3.13 Isolated sketches intended for the Scherzo, 1915

In the 1914 version the twelve-tone theme and its derivatives were absent from these passages. Since mm. 15–34 of the 1915 draft are taken over—with minor alterations—from the earlier version, that could be the case here as well.

However, in the 1915 version Schoenberg attempted to reconcile these two contrasting passages. A comparison of the 1914 and 1915 ver-

Ex. 3.14 mm. 30–1 from the 1915 draft

sions shows Schoenberg was learning how to make his twelve-tone theme, or at least part of it, into the referential basis for the entire composition (see Ex. 3.14). Ex. 3.14 includes mm. 30–1 of the 1915 draft, corresponding to mm. 92–3 in the 1914 version. Neither the melody line nor the accompanying chords display an immediately obvious relationship to the twelve-tone theme. However, in a sketch on the third page of the sketch-book Schoenberg found a way to articulate just such a relationship (see Ex. 3.15).

Ex. 3.15 A sketch that indicates a way of reconciling a segment of the principal theme with a subsidiary idea

What Schoenberg has done is to take the familiar four-note motive, formed from order positions 5–8 of the original transpositional level of the theme, state it in parallel motion with a transposition, and then arpeggiate the result. In the process he has created a way of understanding this seemingly contrasting idea as a derivative of the principal theme of the composition. This reconciliation of contrasting material with the twelve-tone theme marks another important conceptual stage in the development of the serial idea.

At some point in 1915 Schoenberg ceased working on the Scherzo and never returned to complete it. Unfinished though it may be, this movement represents an essential first step in the development of the twelve-tone serial idea. The formation of a twelve-tone theme, the creation of other themes and motives from that theme, the recognition of simple invariants, and, most important of all, the first steps toward the recognition of the abstract serial idea—these are the principal accomplishments of this fragment. To be sure the twelve-tone theme is anything but pervasive and the use of serial transformations elementary, but none the less it is here, in 1914—15, that the serial revolution can properly be said to begin.

Before beginning the Scherzo, Schoenberg had completed three songs for voice and orchestra: Op.22 Nos. 1–3. In July 1916, after stopping work on the Scherzo, Schoenberg returned to finish this opus, and between 19 and 28 July wrote the final song, *Vorgefuehl*. Unlike the Scherzo, this song has no twelve-tone theme, nor is there evidence of serial procedures. That is also the case for two other unfinished works from this period, a chamber piece, from January 1917, and a song, *Liebeslied*, from May of that year, indicating that the twelve-tone and

Ex. 3.16 *Die Jakobsleiter*, mm. 1–6

serial ideas had not yet become central to Schoenberg's compositional thinking.[14]

The next step in Schoenberg's development as a serial composer was his oratorio, *Die Jakobsleiter*. This work was originally intended as the final movement of his great symphony. However, by 1917 he had abandoned the idea of the symphony and had begun to think of this move-ment as an independent composition. The text was written between 1915 and 1917. Serious work on the music began in June 1917 and continued until September 1917, during which period he wrote mm. 1–603.[15] This furious pace of work was interrupted when he was called back into the Austrian army. After his discharge he tried to return to this composition, but over the next five years was only able to write another 100 measures, and he finally abandoned the project in 1922.[16]

The composition opens with a vigorous ostinato in the cellos: C♯ D F E G♯ G. Over this ostinato an arpeggiated chord builds up in the winds and brass, completing the chromatic (see Ex. 3.16). This opening should recall the beginning of the Scherzo. Not only does this movement begin with an ostinato but, once again, with all due deliberation, Schoenberg is careful to present all twelve tones at the beginning of the work.[17]

The similarities do not stop there. In mm. 6–8 Schoenberg builds up to a huge climax as the hexachord of the ostinato is layered in quasi-imitative statements into a powerful crescendo (see Ex. 3.17). The similarities to the passage of canonic imitation in the Scherzo (mm. 32–5) are striking: the simultaneities created between the moving voices are vertical statements of the very hexachord that appears as a line in each of the moving voices. Once again we see Schoenberg experimenting with equating his horizontal and vertical dimensions.

Schoenberg uses the hexachord to create many of the important motives in *Die Jakobsleiter*, just as he indicated in the remarks quoted

[14] Dating and other information about these two fragments can be found in Jan Maegaard, *Studien zur Entwicklung des dodekaphonen Satzes bei Arnold Schönberg*, i. 90–1.

[15] Maegaard discusses the origins and dating of this fragment. See *Studien*, i. 91–3. For a discussion of text/music relationships as evidenced in the sketches see Jean Christensen, 'Schoenberg's Sketches for *Die Jakobsleiter*: A Study of a Special Case", *Journal of the Arnold Schoenberg Institute*, 2 (1978), 112–21.

[16] In 1944 he briefly considered an attempt to complete the work, but this came to nought.

[17] Curiously, Schoenberg remarked many years later that 'When after my retirement from the University of California I wanted to finish *Die Jakobsleiter*, I discovered to my greatest pleasure that this beginning was a real twelve-tone composition. To an ostinato (which I changed a little) the remaining six tones entered gradually, one in every measure'. See 'Composition with Twelve Tones (2)', pp. 247–8. However, given the extensive similarities between the beginning of *Die Jakobsleiter* and the Scherzo (1914), I wonder whether this was really an 'accident'. In all probability Schoenberg, not recalling the relationships to the Scherzo, remembered only the hexachordal basis of *Die Jakobsleiter*, and forgot that he had consciously constructed the opening measures of *Die Jakobsleiter* to include all twelve tones. After all, by the time of Schoenberg's remarks quoted above, more than forty years had elapsed since he had written the beginning measures of *Die Jakobsleiter*.

Ex. 3.17 *Die Jakobsleiter*: hexachordal simultaneities, an extract from m. 8

above. And, as Schoenberg noted, the hexachord is not used as an ordered series: the various motives are formed by reordering the elements of the hexachord.[18]

The use of one hexachord as the source for a number of the principal motives in this work represents a critical conceptual stage in the development of the serial idea. It indicates Schoenberg's interest in forging unity by relating disparate events back to one referential origin, a necessary precondition for the development of serial thinking. The hexachordally derived motives in *Die Jakobsleiter* are a premonition of the exhaustive accountability to a referential ordering that is one of the bases of serial organization.

None the less, however common the hexachordal motives may be, they do not account for anything close to a majority of the musical patterns of the composition. Rather, the hexachordal motives, when they do appear, generally occur as lines in one or more voices. At the same time, the remainder of the fabric might bear little resemblance to the structure of the principal hexachord. Moreover, for long stretches of the composition, no hexachord-derived motives appear at all.

The use of a source hexachord, rather than an ordered series, shows the tentative state of Schoenberg's development of the serial idea. Even

[18] Schoenberg listed some of the themes derived from the hexachord in his essay 'My Evolution', in *Style and Idea*, pp. 88–9.

given the limited use to which this hexachord was put, Schoenberg was unwilling to limit himself to a single ordering. This indicates that although he recognized that the ideal of unity could be achieved by the use of one referential idea, it was not yet clear how this could be accomplished with the exclusive use of one ordering. Several years of learning would be necessary before Schoenberg would be sufficiently skilled in manipulating his series that he could see its potential for generating a wide range of different structures. Only then would he feel confident enough to try to make all the notes of a composition conform to a single referential ordering.

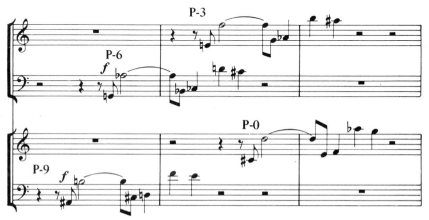

Ex. 3.18 *Die Jakobsleiter*: an extract from mm. 42–4

None the less, some passages in *Die Jakobsleiter* show Schoenberg starting to develop some of the compositional techniques that would eventually permit him to construct a composition from one referential idea. Consider an extract from mm. 42–4 (see Ex. 3.18). Four statements of the hexachord occur in these two measures: P-0, P-3, P-6, and P-9. Since the interval vector for this hexachord is $\{3,2,4,2,2,2\}$ it follows from the common tone theorem that each of the transpositions (3, 6, and 9) holds four notes fixed with respect to each of the other transpositions.[19]

Therefore, at one and the same time, each hexachord can be understood both as a variation and a transposition of the other hexachords. This powerful two-tiered relationship is a model for the kinds of re-

[19] 'Given n pitches or pitch-classes, the $(n^2–n)/2$ non–zero intervals or interval classes they define can be collected in equal interval categories, and the multiplicity of occurrence number associated with each of the categories determines the number of pitches in common between the original collection and the collection transposed by the interval associated with a particular category.' See Babbitt, 'The Structure and Function of Musical Theory', *College Music Symposium*, 5 (1965), 49–60.

lationships that would eventually permit Schoenberg to hold to a referential serial ordering while creating a variety of subsidiary material.

Another feature of the structure of *Die Jakobsleiter* points clearly to the future. With a good deal of consistency, the hexachordally based motives employ the specific pitch-class content of the first appearance of that hexachord: C♯ D E F G G♯. Although transpositions certainly exist, the original transpositional level of the hexachord takes on a referential standing through both extensive temporal emphasis and its appearance in strategic locations in the structure of the composition. This is a premonition of the eventual treatment of the IH-combinatorial complex as a referential region.[20]

Schoenberg's second tour of duty in the Austrian army did not last long, but it was sufficient to break his chain of thought. Although he tried to resume work on *Die Jakobsleiter* after his return, he was not very successful. As the war drew to a close, and social and economic chaos engulfed Austria, Schoenberg found it harder and harder to devote sustained effort to composition. *Die Jakobsleiter* was destined to remain unfinished.

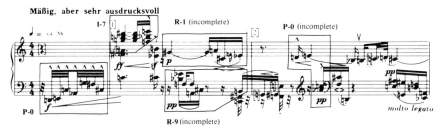

Ex. 3.19 *Klavierstück*, fragment, 1918: occurrences of the referential set

In March 1918 Schoenberg turned away from his unfinished oratorio and sketched out the beginnings of two new compositions: a piano piece and a string septet. Both of these compositions show Schoenberg continuing to think along the lines he had started to develop in the Scherzo and in *Die Jakobsleiter*. The first of these works, a nine-measure fragment of a *Klavierstück*, is dated 9 March 1918.[21]

The work begins with a vigorous thirty-second note figure in the left hand: D E C A♭ G F♯ C♯. If this seven-note line is taken as a referential ordering, then there are several instances of this set in just the first two measures of this fragment[22] (see Ex. 3.19).

---

[20] The structure of the hexachord promotes a referential transpositional level: the hexachord inverts into itself.

[21] The fragment is published in Schoenberg, *Sämtliche Werke*, ed. Josef Rufer et al. (Vienna, 1966), Ser. B, iv. 120–1. A facsimile is printed on p.x.

[22] Moreover, in mm. 5, 6, and 9 there are three further statements (complete and incomplete) of I-7 and P-0.

Schoenberg's choice for his first pair of sets—P-o and I-7—offers still more evidence of his continuing interest in the concept of chromatic completion. But, in contrast to his previous experiments, the chromatic is completed by choosing two set forms, P-o and I-7, whose total pitch-class content completes the chromatic. This is an important discovery: this technique would eventually lead to IH-combinatoriality.

As in the other fragments from this period, the set does not pervade the surface. But Schoenberg's continual preoccupation with these nascent serial ideas was leading him to discover interesting techniques. It would not be long before this accumulated experience would permit him to begin to exploit the potential of serial organization.

A further step in that direction was taken in another incomplete piece from this period. By 9 March 1918, Schoenberg had sketched out some ideas for a string septet.[23] Four days later he made a fair copy of twenty-five measures. The sketches continue on a bit further, but are not worked out—mostly consisting of a single line. In any event the piece was not finished and this very interesting fragment was added to Schoenberg's already lengthy list of incomplete compositions.

In this fragment Schoenberg uses not one principal set but two. They are stated at the same time: one in the first violin from mm. 1–6, the other in the second violin in mm. 1–5 (see Ex. 3.20). Although these are different sets, they do have points in common, the most obvious being that the first five elements of each produces the chromatic pentachord. This property is of particular importance given Schoenberg's treatment of the material, for, after the complete statements of the sets in mm. 1–6, no more complete statements occur. Instead, there are numerous statements of segments of the sets, particularly transpositions of their first pentachords (see Ex. 3.21).

Of additional interest is a sketch-page that shows Schoenberg was also considering passages using other transformations of these sets (see Ex. 3.22). The top four staves on the page merely show various rhythmicizations of complete and partitioned statements of the two principal sets. But on staves 6–7 Schoenberg wrote out P-o of the first set opposite its I-1, and on staves 9–10, P-o of the second set imitated by its I-o.

Neither of these two inversions appear in the draft, but clearly Schoenberg was considering their use. This is yet another sign of the impending serial revolution, for here we have a sketch comprised solely of set material.

The ending of the war did not immediately bring conditions conducive to artistic endeavours. The British naval blockade continued for some time after Versailles in an attempt to ensure compliance with the terms of the treaty, especially payment of reparations. The result was

[23] Dating, and a brief description, can be found in Maegaard, *Studien*, i. 94. Rufer gives a less complete citation: *The Works of Arnold Schoenberg*, trans. Dika Newlin (London, 1962), 110.

Ex. 3.20 String Septet, fragment, 1918: mm. 1–6

Ex. 3.21 String Septet, fragment, 1918: mm. 11–15

Ex. 3.22 String Septet, fragment, 1918: sketches

widespread hunger as well as shortages of virtually everything, particularly coal. In 1919 the only recorded evidence we have of Schoenberg's compositional activity is an eleven-measure fragment of a never-completed song, *Ich fuehle*, from August of that year. There is not enough material here to see if this work would have continued the development of his serial idea.

From this point, until the summer of 1920, there is no further recorded compositional activity.[24] The ideas that Schoenberg had introduced were unrealized. Although the period from 1914–18 saw the first steps towards the development of the twelve-tone method, it was not until 1920 that Schoenberg would have the luxury of uninterrupted time during which he could work out these ideas, experiment with them, and develop some of the techniques that would enable him to begin to see the compositional potential of serial organization.

In none of these pieces does the set pervade the musical structure. That may be the clearest possible sign of the tentative nature of Schoenberg's serial ideas up until 1919. Yet, we have seen in these fragments the first hints of some of the compositional techniques that would eventually permit him to build up an entire composition from one referential ordering. When Schoenberg began composing again in 1920 he would, very quickly, expand those techniques and use them to realize the revolution that he had begun.

---

[24] The Passacaglia, previously thought to date from Mar. 1920, was actually written in March 1926. See my 'Redating Schoenberg's Passacaglia for Orchestra', *Journal of the American Musicological Society*, 40 (1987), 471–94.

4

The Formation of the Twelve-tone Idea, 1920–1923

WITH the benefit of hindsight, many aspects of Schoenberg's twelve-tone method can be seen as logical extensions of the compositional procedures of his previous works. For all the substantive differences between contextual atonality and twelve-tone serialism, it is possible to see the origin of a number of the characteristics of the twelve-tone idea in the compositions between Opp. 11 and 22. Some of the compositional techniques that are found in the contextual compositions, and persist—though transformed—into the twelve-tone period, include: the regulated circulation of all twelve pitch classes with a tendency to complete the chromatic within, or immediately following, phrases; the recurrence of motives or collections that are related to one another by the operations of transposition, inversion, or retrograde; the explicit association of linear and chordal structures. More than enough evidence exists to support the contention that the twelve-tone method was an evolutionary outgrowth of Schoenberg's previous style.

Yet, at a certain point, the evolution of ideas can be revolutionary in effect. No matter how firmly they may be rooted in past practice, a series of gradual changes may have the effect of permitting, even demanding, the development of ideas previously unimaginable, creating a new compositional world that bears little resemblance to its antecedents. Such was the case in that stage of Schoenberg's compositional development in which he began composing 'with twelve tones related only to one another.' The description in Chapter 2 of the integrated compositional procedures of Schoenberg's mature twelve-tone period should indicate that the eventual results of this change were far-reaching in their impact: the musical ideas created by the interaction of set structure with harmony, rhythm, motive, melody, and form were inconceivable in the contextual compositions from Opp. 11–22. Indeed, in its demands on perception, its creation of new modes of continuity, and its reformulation of the concept of musical coherence, the twelve-tone system is revolutionary by any reasonable definition of the term.

Schoenberg's comments, both public and private, give the impression that from the beginning he was aware of the revolutionary character of his compositional discovery. His comment to Josef Rufer, and a similar statement to Erwin Stein, would seem to indicate that he began composing with the twelve-tone system in 1921, making a clean break with previous methods of musical organization.

However, the chronology of the compositions from 1920–3 does not support this picture. Far from displaying a decisive, sudden break with past methods of composition and setting out boldly and immediately in a new direction, Schoenberg's compositional activities of the years 1920–3 reveal a far more gradual process of change. Techniques and methods characteristic of his earlier compositional style persist, coexisting side by side with the new ideas: it took some time for Schoenberg to solve a series of compositional problems and to begin to understand the potential of serial organization.

Any consideration of Schoenberg's stylistic development during the period 1920–3 must be co-ordinated with the complicated chronology of the works from this period. As Maegaard has shown, during the period of the formation of the twelve-tone idea Schoenberg rarely completed even a movement of a composition without interruption.[1] In numerous instances he would begin a composition, write a few measures, and then put the work aside, sometimes for up to three years. In the mean time, he would start, or resume, work on other compositions.

Therefore, in order to understand the evolution of Schoenberg's serial thinking, it will be necessary to follow this complicated chronology as closely as possible. This will entail a certain amount of skipping back and forth from fragment to fragment. As a result, some compositions, like the Suite, Op. 25, will be discussed in several different parts of this chapter. However, the potential confusion of such an approach will be more than offset by the advantage of seeing precisely what Schoenberg had accomplished at each stage in his compositional development during the years 1920–3. Moreover, since there are a number of incomplete compositions from this period, they will be considered as well in order to round out the picture of Schoenberg's compositional thinking during this important stage in the development of his twelve-tone idea.

The disruptions caused by the First World War and the economic and social chaos of its aftermath served to diminish Schoenberg's compositional activities, particularly from late 1917 until the summer of 1920.[2] When Schoenberg resumed writing during that summer, his

---

[1] The convoluted chronology of Schoenberg's early serial period was clarified in Jan Maegaard, 'A Study in the Chronology of op. 23–26 by Arnold Schoenberg', *Dansk aarbog for musikforskning*, 2 (1962). Further information is found in his *Studien zur Entwicklung des dodekaphonen Satzes bei Arnold Schönberg* (Copenhagen, 1972), i. Maegaard corrects many inaccuracies and omissions found in Josef Rufer, *The Works of Arnold Schoenberg*, trans. Dika Newlin (London, 1962).

[2] Schoenberg was called back to the army in Nov. 1917. During that and the following winter he, like the rest of Austria, suffered from a lack of coal and food because of the British blockade. In the period immediately after the war, Schoenberg devoted himself to the rebuilding of cultural life in Austria. He took on numerous students (some without pay) and was deeply involved in the activities of his *Verein*. It is hardly surprising his compositional output suffered. For a summary of

Sehr langsam ($\flat$ = 108)

Ex. 4.1 *Klavierstück*, Op. 23 No. 1: set structure, mm. 1–3

P-0:   F♯ E♭ D F E G   (top voice)
P-5:   B A♭ G B♭ A C   (middle voice; this set is rotated)
RI-2: G B♭ A C B G♯   (middle voice; beginning with G in m. 1)
RI-4: A C B D C♯ (B♭) (bottom voice; set is incomplete)

works immediately start to show the central role that serial organization would play. The compositions from this period reveal a new direction, a different attitude to the structuring of the material.

Although the *Klavierstück*, Op. 23 No. 1, is the first complete composition in which serial ordering is a fundamental principle of organization,
the set is not omnipresent. That very lack of consistency clearly reveals
the limitations of Schoenberg's serial technique at this early stage of
serial composition.

All of the material in the opening phrase, mm. 1–3, can be derived
from a six-note set [3] (see Ex. 4.1). This set, 0 9 8 e t 1, appears—though
somewhat obscurely—in various transformations in all of the voices in
mm. 1–3.[4] The ordered succession, F♯ E♭ D F E G, the top voice in

this period of Schoenberg's life see Hans Heinz Stuckenschmidt, *Schoenberg: His Life, World and
Work*, trans. Humphrey Searle (New York, 1977), 249–62.

[3] There are two fragments—called Opp. 23a and 23b by Maegaard—that must have been written just before the beginning of Op. 23 No. 1 and that clearly contain ideas eventually incorporated into that work. For a transcription and brief commentary see Schoenberg, *Sämtliche Werke*,
ed. Josef Rufer et al, (Vienna, 1966–   ), Ser. B, iv. 122–4. The second of these (no. 11 in the
volume) is, like Op. 24 No. 1, partially serial. There are indications that the *Klavierstück* fragment
numbered 10 may have been meant to be as well, but there is not quite enough material to say for
sure. In No. 11 the upper voice in mm. 1–3 presents a set, transformations of which appear several
more times during the course of the twelve bars of the fragment: P-e, mm. 3–4, P-0, mm. 11–12.
Moreover, segments of this set occur in transposition in numerous places.

[4] The accountability of the three voices to a single referential ordering has been overlooked in
previous discussions of this passage. Jan Maegaard, John Graziano, and Martha Hyde see three
separate and unrelated 'series' in mm. 1–6. See Maegaard, *Studien*, suppl., p.65; John Graziano,
'Serial Procedures in Schoenberg's Op.23', *Current Musicology*, 13 (1972), 58–63; and Hyde, 'Musical Form and The Development of Schoenberg's Twelve-Tone Method', *Journal of Music Theory*,
29 (1985), 89–90. In another analysis, no referential set is seen, but careful and perceptive attention is paid to the 'cells' that pervade this passage. See George Perle, *Serial Composition and Atonality*
(5th edn., Los Angeles, 1981), 10.

mm. 1–3, will be assigned the designation P-o (the D♯ at the end of m. 2 should be thought of as a repetition of the E♭ earlier in the measure).[5] The bottom voice, A C B D C♯, therefore, is an incomplete statement of RI-4, leaving off before what would be the final note of that transformation. Finally, the middle voice can be understood in two ways. The line as a whole, A♭ G B♭ A C B G♯, is a rotation of P-5 yielding the following order-number succession: 1 2 3 4 5 0 1. At the same time, starting with the second note of the line, the succession G B♭ A C B G♯ is a complete statement of RI-2.

This passage is particularly significant because every note relates to a single referential ordering. This is what so clearly distinguishes Op.23 No. 1 from its antecedents, pointing the way toward the serial compositions to come.

A number of aspects of the serial treatment in this passage will figure prominently in Schoenberg's serial technique over the next few years. Moreover, even in these modest beginnings we can see the way in which serial organization starts to transform Schoenberg's compositional thinking.

In the first phrase all twelve pitch classes occur at least once, and no pitch class occurs more than twice.[6] Although the controlled circulation of all twelve pitch classes is a compositional technique that can be traced back at least as far as Op.11 No. 1, its appearance here is more than the continuation of that idea. In this passage the completion of the chromatic is accomplished not by the informal cycling of twelve different pitch classes, but by the choice of set forms for polyphonic combination. This is a crucial distinction, indicating one way in which the serial idea would come to revolutionize Schoenberg's compositional technique.

The three voices of the opening phrase are formed by assigning a set form to each line. This is to become the normative method of generating a polyphonic fabric in the works of the next few years. Three voices

---

[5] The repeated D♯ is very important in a number of local developmental strategies. This is pointed out by Perle, *Serial Composition and Atonality*, p.10. Interestingly, the repetition here recalls a similar event in the fragment Op.23b. In that work the set also appears in the top voice and, similarly, there is a single pitch class repetition in the course of that set statement.

[6] Schoenberg's own analysis of this passage is a case study of the perils involved in uncritically accepting as authoritative a composer's analysis of his own music. Schoenberg asserts that 'The first three measures consist of thirteen tones. Both D and E♭ appear twice, while C♯ is missing'. As his example he gives all of measures 1 and 2 but only the first eighth note from measure 3. This analysis is totally misleading. Schoenberg has stopped the phrase in midstream, cutting across any possible rational phrase boundary. Had he continued the example to the end of measure 3—as the phrasing clearly suggests—the 'missing' C♯ would have been included. Moreover, it is revealing that in the other passages Schoenberg gives as examples of 'how unity is produced by manifold uses of the mutual relations of these tones' the melody of the top voice in mm. 1–3, arbitrarily truncated in his first example, is continued on—in each case—to its logical final note of the phrase, G. See 'My Evolution', in *Style and Idea*, ed. Leonard Stein, trans. Leo Black (New York, 1975), 89–90.

require three different set forms, four voices, four, and so forth. This represents Schoenberg's first attempt to resolve one of the basic challenges of serial organization: How can one produce a polyphonic fabric from a referential linear ordering?

The opening phrase exploits some simple musical invariants. Since the interval series of the P-form is 9 e 3 e 3, that of the RI-form must be 3 e 3 e 9. Therefore, the ordered interval succession, e 3 e, is held invariant between the P- and RI-forms. This property permits the use of a rudimentary version of the two-tiered invariant relationship: sets related by RI are also partially related by T. For example, the succession B♭ A C B in the middle voice—order positions 1–4 of RI-2—is a transposition of the succession E♭ D F E from the top voice. Yet, the two set forms to which these segments belong, are related to one another, not by transposition, but by RI.

The serial consistency of the first three measures is in marked contrast to what follows. From m. 4 until m. 16, no complete statements of the set occur. Rather, Schoenberg proceeds not with serially related set forms, but with the flexible contextual atonality characteristic of his pre-war compositions.[7]

Schoenberg's abandonment of serially formed material in mm. 4–15 is highly revealing. It would seem to indicate that he perceived serial organization to be limited in some important respect, and thus incapable of being used to accomplish certain compositional goals. Therefore, we need to look closely at the passage from mm. 4–15, to see what kind of compositional organization was used in these measures, and to try to understand what this suggests about Schoenberg's serial writing at this stage.

When examined in this light we see that the passage from mm. 4–15 unfolds by means of a continuous process of flexible contextual relationships. By this method of atonal developing variation each chord, line, and harmony results from the subtle alteration and recombination of musical ideas from earlier in the piece.[8]

---

[7] Hyde discusses this work and sees in it an early experiment in serial form. She remarks: 'Repetitions almost always maintain the ordering and contour of the original series and avoid both transposition and inversion. Developmental passages, on the other hand, use unordered sets, which often contain subset structures of the series and frequently use both transposition and inversion. It appears, then, Schoenberg worked out the form of his first serial movement by coordinating his new serial techniques with those of his earlier atonal works.' See 'Musical Form', p.91.

[8] Developing variation was seen by Schoenberg to be one of the most important principles of music since about 1750. In his essay 'Bach' he remarked: 'Music of the homophonic-melodic style of composition, that is, music with a main theme, accompanied by and based on harmony, produces its material by, as I call it, *developing variation*. This means that variation of the features of a basic unit produces all the thematic formulations which provide for fluency, contrasts, variety, logic and unity, on the one hand, and character, mood, expression, and every needed differentiation, on the other hand—thus elaborating the *idea* of the piece.' See *Style and Idea*, p.397. For a thorough summary of Schoenberg's idea of developing variation as well as the critical tradition it

The serial consistency of mm. 1–3, when contrasted with the developing variation of mm. 4–15, suggests that at this early stage of his serial thinking Schoenberg was not yet able to reconcile serial organization with the process of developing variation.[9] Rather, he seems to have thought of the serially formed passage as a point of stability, the source of motivic development. When he needed to continue with a developmental passage he had to turn away from the series to the informal, contextual organization of passages like mm. 4–15.

After m. 16, the composition alternates between serial passages and free development. In the serial passages the set forms used are always those from mm. 1–3 and not any of the other possible transformations.[10] Moreover, the entire polyphonic complex, established in mm. 1–6, is repeated, though varied, several times from mm. 23–31.

Op.23 No. 1, therefore, represents an important stage in the development of the serial idea. On one hand Schoenberg structures the opening phrase so that all the elements relate back to an underlying series, generating the voices with layered set statements. He chooses his transpositions and inversions to provide an approximately even distribution of pitch classes, with chromatic completion an important consideration. This combination of set forms is then fixed for all future statements. On the other hand, this stable complex of set statements was not regarded as sufficiently flexible, nor malleable to provide Schoenberg with the kind of contextual, developmental writing that had been his trademark for nearly thirty years. Serialism to the Schoenberg of Op.23 No. 1 was a device for stability and unity, not yet suitable for the flexible, continuous development of which he was such a master.

The next piece, the *Klavierstück*, Op.23 No. 2 (completed 27 July 1920) has many similar features.[11] The referential serial idea here is a

spawned, see Walter Frisch, *Brahms and the Principle of Developing Variation* (Berkeley, 1984), 1–34. In this book I extend the meaning of Schoenberg's term developing variation to refer not only to motivic development in the strictly homophonic-melodic style of composition, but also to the reformulations, alterations, and transformations of musical ideas in other textures as well. To be sure, with respect to tonal music Schoenberg distinguished between the developing variation of homophonic-melodic music and the 'unravelling' procedures of contrapuntal music. However, given one of the compositional premises of Schoenberg's serial music (the 'unity of musical space') it seems appropriate to apply the idea of developing variation not only to motives stated as lines, but to transformations of musical ideas in the vertical as well as horizontal dimensions.

[9] It is revealing that Schoenberg mentioned the importance of developing variation in his early serial development. He remarked: 'Similarly, as in the case of *Die Jakobsleiter*, here also all main themes had to be transformations of the first phrase. Already here the basic motif was not only productive in furnishing new motif-forms through developing variations, but also in producing more remote formulations based on the unifying effect of one common factor: the repetition of tonal and intervallic relationship.' See 'Composition with Twelve Tones (2)', p.248

[10] mm. 16–18, top voice, P-0; mm. 19–20, bottom voice, RI-4; m. 23, all three voices of mm. 1–3; mm. 26–7, all three voices of mm. 1–3; mm. 29–30, all three voices of mm. 1–3; mm. 30–1, bottom voice, R-0.

[11] Perle sees the first nine notes in the right hand as the principal series and discusses the reappearances of transformations of this series throughout the movement. See *Serial Composition* pp.48–51. Maegaard calls mm. 1–4 'A' and subdivides it into nine subsections. He calls mm. 5–6 'B' and

Ex. 4.2 *Klavierstück*, Op. 23 No. 2: nine-note set, m. 1

nine-note series found in the right hand in m. 1 (see Ex. 4.2). As in the previous piece, the serial idea does not saturate the fabric. Instead Schoenberg proceeds immediately with his characteristic developing variation.

Up to m. 10 there is nothing particularly serial about this composition, for all the material is derived first by this process of development, and then by altered restatement (m. 7 = m. 1; m. 8 = m. 5). Only in m. 10 are there serial aspects to the organization. Starting in this measure is a sequence of transpositions: P-0, P-7, P-2, P-9, and then in m. 12, P-6 and P-4.

The first group of sets—P-0, P-7, P-2, P-9—form a unit, both by virtue of the common transpositional relation (7) and by the sequential surface intervallic and rhythmic patterns. The choice of transpositions has some interesting musical consequences that relate back to the beginning measure.

The bass in m. 1 was formed by systematically extracting—in retrograde—every third note from the set starting at order position 8. This produces the succession C♯ A♭ A. In the restatement of P-0 in m. 10. the bass extracts only two notes, C♯ and A, omitting the A♭. However, when this pattern is transposed up a fifth to P-7, as it is in the second half of m. 10, the succession of pitch classes in the bass is C♯ A A♭, a permutation of the bass line from m. 1 (see Ex. 4.3).

In Op. 23 No. 1 and in the first measures of this movement the *ad hoc* permutation of elements was one of the developmental techniques used by Schoenberg in his non-serial passages to elaborate the musical ideas of the serial motive. However, the permutation of the bass voice motive in m. 10 is no *ad hoc* operation. Rather, it results from the transpositional choice within this measure. By transposing T–7 and extracting only two of the three notes in the bass, leaving out the A♭, a perfect fourth below C♯, Schoenberg ensures that the next note in the bass will complete the trichord from m. 1, at the same time that it functions as part of

subdivides it into thirteen subsections. He then sees the remainder of the movement as a succession of transformations of these subsections. See *Studien*, suppl., pp.66–7. Hyde sees the nine-note set as the referential idea, and once again, notes that the form of the movement is structured by serial techniques similar to those described for the first movement. See 'Musical Form', pp.91–3.

Ex. 4.3 *Klavierstück*, Op. 23 No. 2: transposition yielding a permutation

the next set statement. This systematically derived permutation of a prior event is a prototype for one of Schoenberg's solutions to the problem of the reconciliation between serial order and flexible developing variation.

That Schoenberg was interested in experimenting with serially determined, permutational ideas in this composition is confirmed by the next stage in the serial development. In mm. 13–17, after the sequential transpositions of mm. 10–12, Schoenberg returns to varied restatements of the material from the first nine measures. Then, in both mm. 18 and 19, I-forms of the set are stated in polyphony at three different transpositional levels: in m. 18, I-5, I-9, and I-1; in m. 19, I-3, I-7, and I-e (see Ex. 4.4). Once again, the transpositional relationships are chosen to exploit, systematically, certain permutational features. Schoenberg divides each set into three trichords, thereby highlighting the harmonic equivalence of the second and third trichords (both are pitch-class set 013). Under T-4 and T-8—the intervals of transposition between the voices—the trichords undergo permutation. For example, the B B♭ A♭ of the top voice, the second trichord of I-1, becomes B♭ B G♯, the third trichord of the lowest voice.

Op. 23 No. 2, like its immediate predecessor, has a mixture of serialism and free development. This gives more credence to the supposition

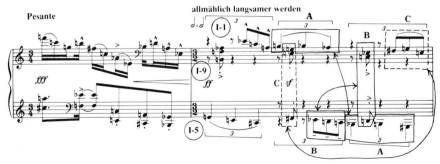

Ex. 4.4 *Klavierstück*, Op. 23 No. 2: trichordal permutation

that at this stage Schoenberg did not saturate the fabric with the series because he did not wish to relinquish the freedom of development characteristic of his contextual period and did not yet see how serial organization could be manipulated to provide that developing variation. However, the tentative experiments with serially determined permutational relationships are the first steps on the road to the ultimate resolution of this paradox.

On 26 July 1920, one day before completing Op. 23 No. 2, Schoenberg began work on what was to be Op. 23 No. 4, writing just fourteen measures before stopping work. He did not return to complete this short composition for nearly three years. This fragment is also a mixture of strictly serial writing and freely structured, contextually organized passages. However, the serial treatment of this piece differs from its predecessors in some important respects.

The principal set of this composition appears in the right hand in m. 1: D♯ B B♭ D E G. And, once again, the set does not account for all events in the composition.

However, in contrast to the first two works from Op. 23, in numerous spots multiple forms of the set occur, sometimes to the point of saturating the surface. Usually, though, these are treated as source collections and not consistently serially ordered (see Ex. 4.5). In the first two

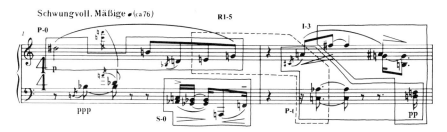

Ex. 4.5 *Klavierstück*, Op. 23 No. 4: set statements, mm. 1–2

measures the set appears no fewer than four times, accounting for everything but the accompaniment in m. 1. However, if the set in the melody in m. 1 is assigned order positions 0–5, then both RI-5, mm. 1–2, and I-3, m. 2, have the order-number succession 0 1 3 2 4 5. Throughout this fourteen-measure fragment unordered, or partially ordered, statements of the set saturate the fabric.[12]

---

[12] Schoenberg made a sketchy analysis of the beginning of this movement, probably when he returned to complete it in 1923. A facsimile of Schoenberg's draft with its analytic markings appears in Hyde, 'Musical Form', p. 101, with a diplomatic transcription by Bryan Simms on the following page. Both Maegaard, *Studien*, suppl., p. 70 and Hyde, 'Musical Form', *passim*, use Schoenberg's analysis as the starting-point for their own. Perle, though not having Schoenberg's analysis at his disposal, came up with similar results. See *Serial Composition*, p. 48.

None the less, not all of the material in this fragment can be related back to the referential series, even in reordered versions. Instead, Schoenberg, as in the other pieces, devised new patterns through the flexible process of developing variation. However, although Schoenberg forms his secondary material by this process, he does not continue with a perpetually unfolding developmental succession. Rather, in the first few measures he creates a few patterns, clearly derived from the original set. These patterns are then fixed and in turn are themselves subjected to serial transformation. For example, the second half of the accompaniment in m. 1, though not a set statement, relates back to some of the essential ideas of the principal set. Not only is its division into three dyads similar to the three dyads of the principal set, but the final four pitch classes are equivalent to a segment of the principal set.

The line, F Eb E G Ab Db in the top voice in mm. 4–5, is not a form of the principal set of the composition. Rather, it is an inversion of the subsidiary idea from the accompaniment in the last half of m. 1. If that subsidiary idea is given the designation S-o (C = o), then this line is its I-1, unordered. Similar passages occur throughout this fragment.

Both the pervasiveness of the principal set and the serialization of the developmental process indicate Schoenberg's interest in having serial organization play a central role in the structure of the composition. However, this is accomplished at the expense of fixed ordering, a throwback to the procedures of *Die Jakobsleiter*. Schoenberg still had not resolved his paradox. Although he seems to have wanted to make the serial idea central to all the events on the surface, he does not seem to have been able to structure the process of flexible developing variation within the bounds of constantly repeating statements of the set.

The next step in Schoenberg's development is of extraordinary significance. Some time before 3 August 1920, and probably after 26 July, Schoenberg began to work on what eventually would become his Serenade, Op.24. Schoenberg started by working out a set of fourteen notes and then used this as the basis of the Variations movement. During this period he almost completed the Variations, with only its coda left unfinished until March 1923.[13]

At approximately the same time Schoenberg sketched ideas for the principal motives of the March, Menuett, Sonett, and *Tanzscene*—i.e. most of the remaining movements of the Serenade, excepting only the *Lied* and Finale. The sketches for all four of these movements are based on the very set Schoenberg used in the Variations.[14] Both this proposed, but later rejected, attempt to base all of the movements on one set and the serial procedures at work in the Variations mark a crucial stage in Schoenberg's serial development.

---

[13] For details of chronology see Maegaard, *Studien*, i. 97–107.
[14] Ibid., suppl., p.4.

The attempt, however fleeting, to base the different movements of the Serenade on a single set gives us another tantalizing clue as to Schoenberg's thinking at this stage in his development. Although by 6 August 1920, when he began working on the *Tanzscene*, it is clear that he had abandoned this idea, its very consideration indicates Schoenberg's interest in extending the set past its use as a local device to become the referential basis of an entire composition.

The Variations from the Serenade represent a significant milestone in Schoenberg's serial development. In this composition he continued to struggle with the problems he had encountered in the other works from this period. But, at the same time he developed some new techniques that were to serve him well in the years to come.

In all of the works from this period there is evidence of Schoenberg's interest in chromatic completion, the antecedent of the aggregate. In the Variations it is the set itself that—almost—includes twelve different pitch classes. The Variations are based on a set of fourteen notes that contains eleven different pitch classes.[15] The chromatic is completed in a number of ways during the course of the movement. In the first variation the guitar adds the missing pitch class as accompaniment to the linear statements of the sets; in the second variation the missing pitch class is appended at the end of linear statements of the set (e.g. guitar, mm. 23–6); in the fourth variation a partitioned statement of the set is combined with a partitioned segment of the retrograde inversion (mm. 47–9). The near completion of the chromatic in the set itself, together with these techniques, ensures that, at least in one dimension, the twelve tones circulate far more consistently in this movement than in any of the other works from this summer.

In the Variations, Schoenberg continues to refine his use of invariants. He structures the set and chooses his set forms in order to exploit certain invariant relationships. The only forms used in this composition are P-0, I-0, and their retrogrades. When these are compared, it can be seen that the content of numerous segments are held invariant[16] (see Ex. 4.6). The structure of the set and the invariants preserved under inversion permit the compositional exploitation of musical relationships that, in a limited and formalized way, resemble the free developing variation of Schoenberg's earlier style. When the linear statement of P-0 at the beginning of the movement is followed in the first variation by a statement of I-0, it is possible to hear I-0 not only as an inversion of the previous set statement but, also, as a variant in which specific com-

[15] On the sketch-page for the set of this work the set is laid out with the pitch class that completes the chromatic appended after the fourteenth note of the set. See the facsimile ibid., 97.

[16] The structure of the set and the invariants produced are discussed in Joel Lester, 'Pitch Structure Articulation in the Variations of Schoenberg's Serenade', *Perspectives of New Music*, 6 (1968), 22–34.

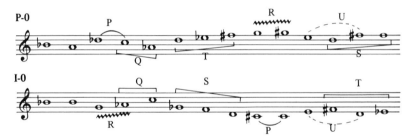

Ex. 4.6 Invariant segments in the set of the variations

ponents of P-0 are reordered. This is an accomplishment of great importance, for we see Schoenberg learning how to make the structure and choice of sets fulfil functions previously assigned to non-serial developing variation.

One of the most significant characteristics of the Variations is their near-total adherence to the serial ordering. Whereas other compositions from this period treat the set as an occasional device, to be abandoned when necessary, in this movement almost every note can be understood as part of a set statement. This means that unlike the other compositions Schoenberg attempted to structure the development entirely in serial terms—he did not abandon the series, as he did in Op. 23 Nos. 1 and 2, in order to proceed with developing variation.

A sketch-page, showing Schoenberg's set forms for this movement, contains the pre-compositional preparation for another technique that has great significance both for this piece and for Schoenberg's twelve-tone method (see Ex. 4.7). After writing out the set forms to be used, Schoenberg presents these same four forms, each partitioned to produce a three-voice counterpoint.

In the second variation this partitioning appears at the beginning of the variation, first in mm. 23–4 and then again in mm. 27–8 (see Ex. 4.8). Schoenberg arranges the chords to exploit the invariant properties described in Ex. 4.6: two of the chords are held invariant. The formation of these chords from the referential linear ordering is merely the first step in the developmental process. As a result of the partitioning of the set into three voices, new lines are created that are not segments of the set. The succession F E F♯ G♯ A in the violin in mm. 23–4 represents order positions 14, 11, 8, 5, and 2 from R-0[17] (see the top voice in the partitioned set form marked TK in Schoenberg's sketch in Ex. 4.7).[18]

[17] In Schoenberg's sketch he assigns order numbers from 1–14 to the notes of the set. Therefore, in this discussion, order numbers will begin with 1, in keeping with Schoenberg's numbering. However, throughout the rest of this book, order numbers start with 0.

[18] TK = *Thema Krebs*, i.e. the theme (set) in retrograde.

Ex. 4.7 Partitioning of the set forms for the variations in Schoenberg's sketches

Ex. 4.8 The partitionings of Ex. 4.7 as they appear in the second variation, mm. 23–8

The next stage in the developmental process occurs in the fourth variation. The partitioned lines now appear as independent events. For example, in mm. 49–52, I-o appears partitioned into the three voices of the sketch-page. However, the lines are no longer aligned so as to preserve the original ordering of the set. Moreover, in the violin the succession F E F♯ G♯ A from R-o occurs, but this pentachord is not part of a complete statement of R-o or any other set form. Rather, it is a melodic pattern that has been created as the result of a process of development that included a series of steps: from set, to chords derived from that set, to lines created by the voices of the chords. These formalized variations may not be as flexible nor as subtle as the developing variation of his free contextual writing, but step by step Schoenberg is solving compositional problems and learning how to replicate his flexible developing variation within a serial context.

Another technique of great importance makes its first appearance in this movement: isomorphic partitioning. At the beginning of the third variation Schoenberg takes the first nine order positions of P-o and partitions them between the clarinet and mandolin. In the following measure the identical assignment of order positions is applied to the statement of I-o appearing in the bass clarinet and violin (see Ex. 4.9). Furthermore, this produces an invariant segment, for when order positions 3 4 5 9 are partitioned out of P-o and I-o, the resultant segments are retrogrades of one another.

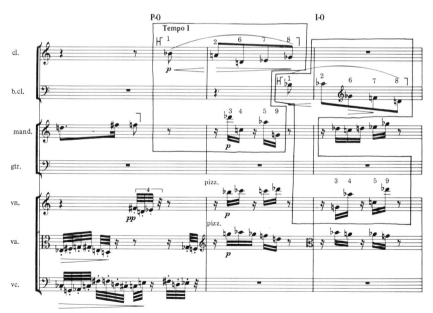

Ex. 4.9 Isomorphic partitioning, third variation, mm. 34–6

The Variations represent a significant advance in the scope and consistency of Schoenberg's serial technique. Not only was he capable of sustaining serially related ideas throughout an entire movement but also he started to develop a number of techniques that would permit serial relationships to substitute for the functions previously fulfilled by the informal procedures of developing variation. It would not be long before the techniques learned here would be refined and polished so that he would be able to follow the series, but none the less, write as freely as before.

Schoenberg closed this season of intense compositional activity with work on several other movements meant for the Serenade. Two of these movements, the so-called Op.24a and Op.24b would never be completed.[19] The third, the *Tanzscene*, was begun this summer, but not completed until 1923.

These three fragments are important as much for what they omit as for what they include. In the four previous movements from the summer of 1920 there was a steady increase in accountability to the referential series, culminating with the Variations in which virtually every note related back to the fourteen-note set. This might give the impression that Schoenberg was progressing steadily to a solution of the serial dilemma and felt ready to have the set become the sole referential basis for his compositions. The compositional organization of these three fragments shows that was not yet the case, giving instead a clear indication of the limitations of Schoenberg's serial thinking at this early stage of his development.

Both the *Tanzscene* and Op.24a are organized much like the three movements from Op.23 from earlier in the summer.[20] They have principal sets, but in neither case do those sets saturate the surface. Rather, there is the same mix of serial organization and free developing variation that Schoenberg employed in those earlier compositions.[21] The very fact of their inconsistent serial organization gives proof that Schoenberg, in the summer of 1920, had not yet overcome the perceived limitations of serial organization and was not yet ready to entrust all of his compositional ideas to this method.

Following the intense activity of the summer of 1920 Schoenberg was unable to devote time to composition until the following summer which he spent at Traunkirchen. However, instead of returning to the numerous compositions left unfinished from the previous season, Schoenberg began a new set of piano pieces, a set that would become the Suite,

[19] The two fragments are transcribed in Maegaard, *Studien*, suppl., pp.60–4.

[20] Op.24*b* is so short that it is not really possible to make reliable conclusions about its organization.

[21] Schoenberg gives a brief example from the *Tanzscene* showing how he derives the accompaniment of the *Valse* part by rearranging the tones of the first measure and how he completes the chromatic with the notes of the clarinet line. See 'My Evolution', *Style and Idea*, p.90.

Op. 25. When he started working on this composition he called it *Series II*, apparently thinking of Op. 23 as *Series I*. The movements he worked on, the Prelude and Intermezzo, were numbered '1' and '2' and there is no evidence at that stage that Schoenberg was thinking of these pieces as parts of a neo-baroque suite.

From 24–9 July 1921 Schoenberg worked on and completed the Prelude. By 25 July he had also begun work on the Intermezzo, but wrote only ten measures before setting it aside. He did not return to finish the Intermezzo until February 1923.

Although later layers of the Suite are unquestionably based on a linearly ordered twelve-tone set, that is not the case for that part of Op. 25 that was written in the summer of 1921. Rather, the Prelude and the Intermezzo are based on three tetrachords which together make up an aggregate. Although each is internally ordered, the ordering between them is not necessarily precompositionally determined. This is confirmed by both Schoenberg's sketches, where the evolution of this tritetrachordal complex is quite clear, and by his set tables, where the referential material is plainly laid out as a polyphonic complex of tetrachords[22] (see Ex. 4.10).

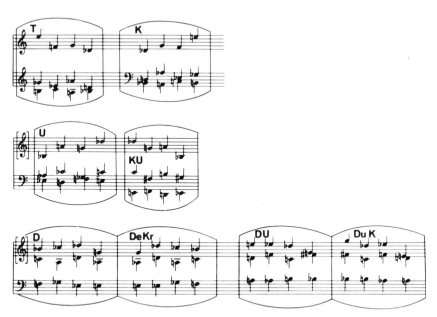

Ex. 4.10 Set tables for Op. 25

[22] Schoenberg's sketches for the Suite reveal that his initial referential idea was a three-voice, aggregate-completing complex, with five elements in one voice, four in another, and three in the last. Gradually, he altered his initial idea to the form it took in the Suite. See *Sämtliche Werke*, ser. B, iv. 68–77.

All of this indicates that at the very first stages of the Suite Schoenberg did not have in mind a referential *linear* ordering of all twelve pitch classes, but rather, a polyphonic, tetrachordal, aggregate forming complex. This hypothesis receives added support not only from the music but, paradoxically, from another sketch-sheet where Schoenberg does write out the three tetrachords in a linear ordering.[23]

In this sketch-sheet the set is linearly ordered, to be sure, but the critical information is not given by the prime form, but rather by the retrograde. Instead of starting with order position e and regressing to 0, Schoenberg has the following order-position pattern: 3 2 1 0 / 7 6 5 4 / e t 9 8. That is, the order of the tetrachords is preserved and the retrogression occurs entirely within the tetrachords. Therefore, this 'retrograde' is produced not by the application of the classical operation of retrograde to a linear statement of P-0 but, rather, by applying retrograde to each of the tetrachords in the polyphonic complex and then stating the tetrachords in succession. This evidence, plus that provided by the other sketches together with the musical organization of the Prelude and Intermezzo fragment, shows that in 1921 the referential idea for this work was the three-voice tetrachordal complex and not a linear ordering of the twelve tones.[24]

Schoenberg limited the transformations to four (with their retrogrades): P-0, P-6, I-0, and I-6, although there is evidence that he considered others.[25] These specific transformations fostered a useful array of invariant and developmental relationships. The exploitation of these relationships is the great accomplishment of this composition, an indi-

---

[23] A transcription of Schoenberg's sketch is printed ibid., iv. 76.

[24] The view that the 1921 layer of Op.25 is not based on a linear ordering of the twelve tones is also held by Maegaard and Brinkmann. See Maegaard, 'A Study in the Chronology', p.110 and Brinkmann (ed)., Schoenberg, *Sämtliche Werke*, Ser. B, iv. 67. On the other hand, Hyde takes the view that the linear ordering of the twelve tones is the referential idea, even in 1921. However, that view is not supported by the music, sketches, or set tables from that year. In the 1921 layer the set appears in linear form just three times, all of them in the Prelude. In two of the cases (mm. 1–3, r.h. and mm. 7–8, l.h.) the twelve tones are indeed linearized in precisely the ordering that Hyde takes to be the referential linear ordering. But, in the third case, mm. 10–11, r.h., Schoenberg presents the set in his peculiar retrograde. This transformation cannot be derived from those other orderings by any of the classic operations. Indeed, this ordering with the order-number sequence 3 2 1 0 / 7 6 5 4 / e t 9 8 cannot be derived from the other ordering by the operation of retrograde. Therefore, no single referential linear ordering can be deduced from the Prelude. Moreover, no one presented only with the Intermezzo could deduce *any* referential linear ordering of the twelve tones, let alone the two, somewhat contradictory orderings derivable from the Prelude. (But, that is not the case for the final two pieces written in 1923, as we shall see below.) The lack of a recognized referential linear ordering of the twelve tones for the 1921 layer of this piece should call into question some of Hyde's conclusions. In 'Musical Form' she repeats and amplifies observations made in earlier papers. That is, the ordering of the set of Op.25 was decided upon because combinations of P-0, I-0, P-6, and I-6 produce more invariants equivalent to harmonies embedded in the set than the other orderings considered by Schoenberg. However, those harmonies are calculated from twelve-tone linear orderings of those sets, none of which is so ordered in the sketches. And—until 1923—no linear serial ordering was treated as the referential basis of this composition.

[25] *Sämtliche Werke*, ser. B, iv. 76.

cation of Schoenberg's growing ability to have serially consistent material reflect the kind of developmental progression characteristic of his contextual compositions. The structure of the tetrachords and the relationships between them control the developmental process.

The opening of the Prelude offers some typical examples. In the first measure and a half the right hand states the first two tetrachords of P-o while the left hand, starting later and moving slower, unfolds the first tetrachord of P-6 (see Ex. 4.11). The registral placement of the pitch

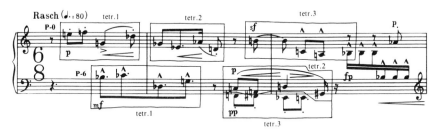

Ex. 4.11 Prelude from the Suite, Op. 25, mm. 1–3

classes of P-6 are chosen to suggest canonic imitation, a feature that persists into the second tetrachord. By placing the first two pitches of P-6 against the last two pitches of the first tetrachord of P-o Schoenberg creates the tetrachord G B♭ C♭ D♭. This is equivalent, by content, to the first tetrachord of P-6, thus intimating the continuation in the left hand. Because of the common tones G and D♭ it is possible to hear the first tetrachord of P-6 not only as a canonic imitation of P-o but, also, as a reshaping, a development, as two new tones, B♭ and C♭, are associated with the fixed ones, G and D♭. A similar structure is created in the second measure where the combination of the first two notes of the second tetrachord of P-o and the last two notes of the first tetrachord of P-6 yields the tetrachord G♭ E♭ D♭ G, a tetrachord (pitch-class set 0146) equivalent to the second tetrachord of the set.

The continuation into mm. 2–3 displays a particularly rich array of relationships that are at once serial and variational. The second tetrachord of P-o in the right hand of m. 2 is imitated at the tritone by the corresponding tetrachord of P-6 from mm. 2–3. The choice of register here emphasizes the canonic imitation, as the registral relationships of the right hand are strictly imitated in the left hand.

However, there is another way of understanding the relationship between these two tetrachords. Because of the tritone transposition, the dyad A♭–D from P-o is preserved in P-6. Thus, it is possible to hear the second tetrachord of P-6 both as a transposition of the equivalent tetrachord in P-o and as a reworking, in which the A♭–D dyad is held fixed, reversed in order and associated with two new pitch classes.

If the second tetrachord of P-6 can be understood to originate, at least on one level, as a reworking of the elements of the second tetrachord of P-o, then in a similar fashion the final tetrachord of P-o can be seen as both a transposition of the final tetrachord of P-6 and as a flexible reshaping of the second tetrachord of P-6.

The succession B C A B♭ in the right hand is, of course, a tritone transposition of the bottom line in the left hand in mm. 2–3. Yet, at the same time, its C A imitates the C A from the left hand at the end of m. 2. Moreover, Schoenberg has arranged the rhythmic position of these two dyads to emphasize their invariance.[26]

Schoenberg also exploits the ordering characteristics of the final tetrachord to effect a fusion of developing variation and serial order. A typical and particularly felicitous example is offered by mm. 3–5 (see Ex. 4.12). Here there are successive statements of I-6 (mm. 3–5) and R-6 (m. 5), that is, two RI-related set forms. Under RI the tetrachord E♭ D F E from I-6 (middle voice, m. 4) becomes E E♭ F♯ F in R–6 (bottom voice, m. 5). However, the symmetrical interval ordering of the final tetrachord allows another interpretation: this can also be understood as a transposition up a semitone. This interpretation is supported by the dynamics, where the *sf* on F in m. 4 is paralleled by the accent mark on F♯ in m. 5.

Ex. 4.12   RI-relationships reinterpreted as transpositions

Once the transpositional relationship between these tetrachords is recognized it permits a reinterpretation of the relationship between I-6 and R-6. R-6 can now be understood both as a serial transformation and as a varied transposition. Thus B♭-A (left hand m. 3–4) becomes C♭-B♭ (upper voice, m. 5); A♭-C♭ (upper voice, mm. 3–4) becomes A-C (middle voice, m. 5); G♭-C (top voice, m. 4) becomes G-D♭ (right hand, m. 5).

---

[26] The invariant properties of the two set forms, as well as the metric consequences of that invariance, are discussed in David Lewin, 'A Theory of Segmental Association', *Perspectives of New Music*, 1 (1962), 93–4.

In sum, every discrete dyad of R-6 can be seen to be a transposition of the dyads from I-6. This enables us to understand R-6 both as a serial transformation (RI-related) and a varied transposition. Schoenberg has discovered one way to manipulate serially related events to create the free developing variation of his contextual compositions.

The opening of the Intermezzo offers a good example of Schoenberg's exploitation of the common subsets between the different tetrachords (see Ex. 4.13). The first chord of the movement is F Db E, order positions 013 from the first tetrachord of P-0. This is a 014 trichord, a pitch-class set that is one of the common subsets of the first and second tetrachords. In m. 2, after the ritenuto, Schoenberg continues with I-6, but this time the drone chord is formed from the second tetrachord. Yet here, too, the extracted trichord is pitch-class set 014.

Ex. 4.13 Common 014 trichords suggesting transposition

Schoenberg emphasizes this relationship by the distribution of pitches. The registral disposition of the 014 trichord from I-6 is identical to that of the equivalent subset in P-0. The trichordal invariance permits us to understand this passage as both a serial transformation of one tetrachord in P-0 and a varied transposition of another.

That part of the Suite, Op.25, written in the summer of 1921, represents a giant step forward in Schoenberg's serial abilities. In this movement and a third Schoenberg discovered some of the important compositional techniques that were to figure prominently in his music in the years to come. Above all, we can see his first successful attempts to reconcile the seemingly contradictory tendencies of serial consistency and developing variation. This reconciliation is all the more significant in that the medium through which it was carried out was the structure of the referential set.

When Schoenberg returned to Vienna from Traunkirchen, after his summer of vacation and composition, he was able—unlike the previous year—to continue composing through the remainder of 1921 and into 1922. He began by working on the March from the Serenade, a movement whose earliest ideas had appeared in 1920. When Schoenberg returned to this work in September 1921, he kept the rhythm and contour of the earlier sketch, but supplied a new set of pitches.

In the March Schoenberg continued to refine his serial technique. Although this work is not consistently serial, the set is used in a number of different ways and is treated to some interesting developments, including the elegant use of isomorphic partitioning (mm. 9–15 and 25–31).

After completing the March Schoenberg turned to the Menuett (begun October 1921 but not completed until 1923). Then, in the first half of 1922, he sketched ideas for several new compositions, none of which was completed: a violin concerto and several chamber works.[27] All of these works are based on sets of varying lengths. From the techniques displayed in these fragments it is clear that Schoenberg was continuing to work with serial techniques much in the manner of the other compositions of this period.

By July 1922, Opp. 23–5 were all in progress, though none of the cycles was finished. But all of these incomplete fragments were dwarfed by the *Die Jakobsleiter* fragment, begun five years earlier.

In July 1922 Schoenberg took up the *Die Jakobsleiter* once again and tried to finish it. He worked on it for some time, wrote fewer than 100 more measures, but then gave up. By the following year it was clear that the work would remain unfinished.[28]

That part of *Die Jakobsleiter* written in 1922 is not markedly different from the earlier section written in 1917. Once again the source hexachord appears frequently, always stated as a line, most often at the original level of transposition. If there is a difference between this layer of *Die Jakobsleiter* and the 1917 layer it is that the principal set occurs more often, sometimes with several set forms appearing in several voices at once.

However, except for the increased frequency of appearance of the principal hexachord, there are few signs of the intervening years of serial experience. By and large Schoenberg seems to have returned to the compositional thinking of the earlier period. Perhaps that is one of the reasons why this work was never completed. By 1922 Schoenberg

---

[27] Transcriptions of the sketches for these works are in Maegaard, *Studien*, suppl., pp.56–8.

[28] In a letter to Zemlinsky, dated 12 Feb. 1923, Schoenberg indicated that he considered the interruption permanent. See Arnold Schoenberg, *Briefe*, ed. Erwin Stein (Mainz, 1958), 84.

was seriously exploring the compositional possibilities of serial ordering. He was so excited about his new method he confided to several people that he had discovered something so important that it would transform German music for the next century. In order to finish *Die Jakobsleiter* and keep it stylistically consistent he would have had to suspend his serial development for quite some time and would have had to return to the compositional thinking of a prior period of his stylistic development. Schoenberg's abandonment of *Die Jakobsleiter* in 1922 may be the clearest possible mark of how important serial organization had become in his compositional thinking.[29]

After giving up on *Die Jakobsleiter* Schoenberg turned his attention back to the Serenade. He started to work on one of the movements whose opening idea had been sketched two years earlier: the Sonett. He wrote out the entire melodic line and the first twelve measures— enough to serve as a model for the complete composition. He then stopped work on the Sonett, not returning to finish it until March 1923.

As was the case with the March the contour and rhythm of the melodic idea from 1920 were preserved, but supplied with a new set of pitches. In altering the set, he changed it from the fourteen-note set of 1920 to a twelve tone set, with all pitch classes represented. Although the ordering of the set would be changed again in 1923 the basic elements of Schoenberg's compositional design were established in 1922.

Schoenberg set a German translation of a Petrarch sonnet which preserves the original number of syllables in each line: eleven. Since the voice presents the set as a line with one note per syllable, at the end of the first line of text the last note of the set is left over. That 'extra' note becomes the first note in the setting of the second line of text. Schoenberg then continues with ten order positions from a second statement of P-o. The third line of text begins with the last two notes of P-o and continues on through the first nine notes of the next statement of P-o. In a similar fashion Schoenberg proceeds through the text. This results in rotated set statements, a characteristic feature in the early serial period (see Ex. 4.14).

In his early serial compositions Schoenberg customarily generated the polyphonic fabric by layering different set statements, one per voice. However, the first sketches for the Sonett show Schoenberg beginning to think about other ways of producing a polyphonic twelve-tone fabric. The solution of the Sonett may be somewhat simplistic, but it lays the groundwork for the powerful multidimensional set presentations of Schoenberg's mature period.[30]

[29] A similar view of Schoenberg's reasons for abandoning *Die Jakobsleiter* is advanced in Winfried Zillig, 'Notes on Arnold Schoenberg's Unfinished Oratorio "Die Jakobsleiter,"'*Score*, 25 (1959), p. 14.

[30] Schoenberg himself was somewhat apologetic about this work: 'The fourth movement, "Sonett," is a real "composition with twelve tones." The technique is here relatively primitive,

Ex. 4.14 The vocal line of the Sonett in the 1922 version

At the same time the vocal line presents a continually rotating succession of statements of P-o, the accompaniment is structured so that the first few notes in the melody line together with the other voices form a local, partitioned version of P-o (see Ex. 4.15).

This is the first instance of a multidimensional set presentation; there are clearly defined levels of hierarchy. On one level the vocal line presents a succession of rotated statements of P-o. These middleground set presentations are supported by local, partitioned statements of the same set form.[31]

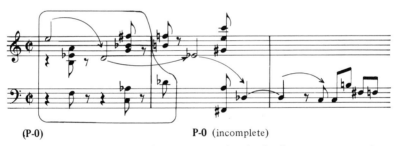

Ex. 4.15 Multidimensional set presentation in the Sonett, 1922 version

By the standards of his later multidimensional set presentations, this solution is somewhat ingenuous. Schoenberg has achieved a multidimensional set presentation, but at the risk of developmental stasis. In the completed version of this movement, one set form, P-o, appears constantly, both horizontally and vertically: no other forms occur. Thus there is no real development, just a continual, formalized rotation of the set.

because it was one of the first works written strictly in harmony with this method.' This quote is from a letter Schoenberg wrote to Nicolas Slonimsky in response to the latter's request for information about the origins of the twelve-tone method. See his *Music Since 1900* (4th edn., New York, 1971), 1316.

[31] Actually, as can be seen from the example, Schoenberg only hinted at this solution in 1922: only one of the supportive set statements is complete. However, since this matches up exactly with what he did when he returned to the work the following year, I am assuming that the multidimensional idea was present here, even though there is not quite enough evidence to be absolutely certain that is the case.

None the less, the Sonett represents another major leap forward in Schoenberg's serial thinking. In the sketches for this piece we see the first attempts to manipulate the set so that it controls not just one dimension of the musical surface, but several.

Four months later, in February 1923, Schoenberg began an intense, largely unbroken period of compositional activity. By 14 April 1923, Opp. 23, 24, and 25 would be complete and Schoenberg would be ready to begin his first large-scale twelve-tone composition, the Wind Quintet, Op. 26.

Schoenberg, under some pressure to finish these compositions and deliver them to his publishers, first turned to the set of piano pieces, Op. 23. By 6 February 1923 he had begun (or resumed)[32] work on Op. 23 No. 3, completing it three days later. A day later he turned back to the unfinished fragment Op. 23 No. 4, completing it in three days. He then started to work on the last piece of this set, Op. 23 No. 5, the Waltz. The entire set was completed by 17 February 1923.

The *Klavierstück*, Op. 23 No. 3, is based on a five-note set: 0 4 6 1 3. As in almost all of the serial compositions up to this point, the set does not account for all events on the surface. Rather, there is a mixture of serial and contextual organization.[33] However, in some places in this piece, in particularly clever ways Schoenberg arranges the succession of set forms so that they supersaturate the surface.[34]

A characteristic example of this method of organization is provided by the opening few measures (see Ex. 4.16). In the first three measures both ordered and unordered set statements account for almost every note on the surface. In several cases notes function as elements in more than one set form. Schoenberg was able to supersaturate the surface with set forms because of certain properties of the set: at two different transpositions of I four notes are held invariant.[35] This feature determines much of the local set succession. Since P-0 has four notes in common with both I-7 and I-4, overlapping set statements require the

---

[32] Maegaard, though he admits that the dating seem straightforward, suggests that it is possible, even probable, that Op. 23 No. 3 was begun earlier than 1923, perhaps as early as Nov. 1921. See *Studien*, i. 96. In a later article Maegaard discusses this problem more thoroughly, restating his doubts about the 1923 date. See 'Om den kronologiske placering af Schönbergs klaverstykke op. 23 nr. 3', *Musik en forskning*, 2 (1976), 5–10. Similarly, and for identical reasons, Hans Oesch expresses doubts about the 1923 dating of this work. See his 'Schönberg im Vorfeld der Dodekaphonie', *Melos*, 41 (1974), 330–8. However, since Schoenberg wrote very little serial music in 1922 (in that year Schoenberg worked mainly on *Die Jakobsleiter*), redating the beginning of Schoenberg's work on Op. 23 No. 3 to the end of 1921 would not substantively change the chronological picture of Schoenberg's stylistic development outlined in the present book.

[33] This piece has received a good deal of intensive analytical attention. See Perle, *Serial Composition*, pp. 45–7; Maegaard, *Studien*, suppl., pp. 67–9; Babbitt, 'Since Schoenberg', pp. 3–6; Oesch, 'Schönberg im Vorfeld', pp. 330–8; Hyde, 'Musical Form', pp. 93–5.

[34] See for example Babbitt's discussion of m. 18, 'Since Schoenberg', pp. 3–6 and Ex. 64, Perle, *Serial Composition*, p. 47.

[35] Some of Schoenberg's experiments with the set are preserved in his sketches. See *Sämtliche Werke*, ser. B, iv. 60–1. Note that Schoenberg has worked out the serial basis for m. 2. He then added a note saying that he had written this sketch after composing the work.

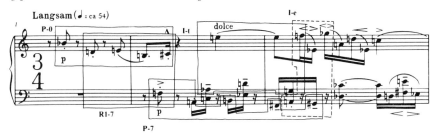

Ex. 4.16 *Klavierstück*, Op. 23 No. 3: set saturation, mm. 1–3

addition of but one additional note. For instance, when the left hand in m. 2 starts a statement of P-7 with the note F, this note, together with the last four elements of P-0 makes an overlapping statement of RI-7.[36]

Another property of this set recalls the set of the Suite, Op. 25. The interval ordering of the set of Op. 23 No. 3 is 4 2 7 2. Therefore, the interval ordering of the retrograde inversion is 2 7 2 4. Since the last three intervals of the prime form are the same as the first three of the RI-form it is possible to understand the RI-form as both a varied transposition and a retrograde inversion of the prime form. Thus, just as in Op. 25, the structure of Schoenberg's set directs the development.

In all of the compositions of this period there is ample evidence of Schoenberg's concern for chromatic completion. Most often the chromatic was completed in an *ad hoc* fashion, dependent neither on the structure of the set nor on the particular combination of set forms. Sometimes, however, as in the Variations from the Serenade and in the Suite, Op. 25, chromatic completion was built into the referential set itself. Other times, as in Op. 23 No 1, it was the combination of particular set forms that completed the chromatic. These two latter methods are important for Schoenberg's development because, eventually, they will be transformed into the twelve-tone set and the compositional aggregate.

The set of Op. 23 No. 3 has the property that P-0 has pitch classes in common with every transformation except one, I-e. Therefore, when those two forms are combined, ten of the twelve pitch classes of the chromatic result. Schoenberg exploits this property to create an aggregate (see Ex. 4.17). In mm. 26–7 P-0 and I-e are combined in a kind of fourth species counterpoint. The combination of these two set forms includes all pitch classes except for C and G. At the end of m. 27 the two voices continue on immediately to the dyad C and G thus completing the aggregate in this pair of voices.[37]

Another instance of systematic aggregate construction is the fascinat-

---

[36] The intersection of content between P-0 and I-7 produces a 013467 hexachord. This hexachord plays a central role in the development. See Babbitt, 'Since Schoenberg', pp. 3–6.

[37] Ibid., 5.

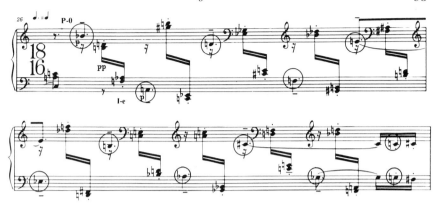

Ex. 4.17 *Klavierstück*, Op. 23 No. 3: aggregate formation, mm. 26–7

ing passage from the end of m. 18 to m. 19 (see Ex. 4.18). Schoenberg has arranged a maze of transformations of the set so that they pervade the surface. One of the consequences of this is that the left hand strings together four 048 trichords to produce an aggregate.[38]

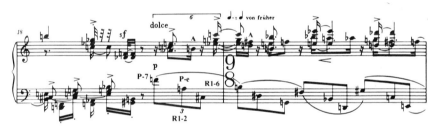

Ex. 4.18 *Klavierstück*, Op. 23 No. 3: aggregate formation, mm. 18–19

(Because of the complexity of the overlapping set statements, the set forms are indicated by placing their label next to the first note of each set form)

In these two examples the chromatic is completed, not by *ad hoc* procedures, with free repetitions of the tones, but, rather, by the controlled, systematic selection of set forms. These are true aggregates—not instances of informal chromatic completion.

Moreover, the selection of set forms had to be determined by the structure of the set. This is a crucial conceptual breakthrough and will have profound ramifications for Schoenberg's development. Schoenberg has begun to recognize how to make the structure of the set a compositional determinant that suggests norms of set combination.

Schoenberg next turned his attention to Op. 23 No. 4, left incomplete for nearly three years. Although his serial technique had developed far

[38] Babbitt gives this passage a brilliant analysis, ibid., 3–4.

past the level of this fragment during the intervening period, he was able to return to the procedures of that earlier period and complete the work in the same style with which it had begun. This was possible primarily because there are a number of measures in the second half of the composition that are nearly literal reworkings of measures from the first half of the composition (mm. 1–2 = mm. 20–1 and 24–5; mm. 4–5 = mm. 26–7).

Upon completing Op.23 No. 4 Schoenberg started work on the last piece of Op.23, the Waltz. This composition is based on a twelve-tone set: C♯ A B G A♭ F♯ A♯ D E E♭ C F. With one exception (R-0 in mm. 104–6), P-0 is the only set form used.

Most discussions of the Waltz have commented on the elementary level of its twelve-tone technique. However, it would be a mistake to dismiss this work out of hand. In this piece Schoenberg devises interesting solutions to some of the problems he had faced since the beginning of his serial period.

We know from some hints in Schoenberg's writings that he was concerned with the problem of building an entire piece from one set. He remarked:

In the first works in which I employed this method, I was not yet convinced that the exclusive use of one set would not result in monotony. Would it allow the creation of a sufficient number of characteristically differentiated themes, phrases, motives, sentences, and other forms? At this time, I used complicated devices to assure variety.[39]

In the Waltz Schoenberg set for himself the challenge of building an entire composition from very limited material: one set form. In the process of meeting this compositional challenge he developed ways of manipulating his material in some interesting, and yes, even subtle, ways.

Schoenberg assured sufficient variety by avoiding the regular congruence of phrases and set statements. For example, the phrase in mm. 8–13 begins with the last two elements of one set statement, proceeds through two more complete statements and the first five elements of a third. Thus, neither the beginning nor the end of this phrase is coincidental with the beginning or the end of a set statement. Moreover, the set forms do not mark off the subdivisions within the phrase. Because of this constant alteration of the material used to initiate and conclude phrases and phrase subdivisions, Schoenberg ensures that there will be no ostinato-like repetitiveness.

Yet, it would be a serious underestimation of Schoenberg's compositional abilities to presume that he was merely after a compositional realization of the old bromide 'variety within unity'. Rather, even

[39] 'Composition with Twelve Tones (1)', p.224.

within the confines of this repetitive serial ordering, Schoenberg found a way to replicate some of the free-flowing development of his earlier, non-serial works. A good way to understand this is by comparing two similar passages: mm. 22–7 of the Waltz and mm. 1–3 from Op.23 No. 2, written almost three years earlier (see Ex. 4.19).

In Op.23 No. 2 (see Ex. 4.2, above), the opening measures proceed by a flexible and informal process of developing variation. The second

Ex. 4.19 Developing variation in the Waltz, mm. 22–7

phrase varies the ideas of the opening phrase by means of the *ad hoc* permutation of its elements and the controlled addition of other tones.

Compare that with the remarkably similar passage from Op.23 No. 5. Because the first phrase (mm. 22–3) spans a total of fourteen order-positions beginning with the first element of the set, the next phrase (mm. 24–5) must begin with the third element. By holding rhythm, articulation, contour, and durations fixed, Schoenberg highlights these two as parallel passages. But, because events in equivalent metric positions are from different points in their respective set statements, Schoenberg manages to create a developmental dynamic. For instance, the last three of the four sixteenth-note dyads from the first statement appear at the beginning of the second phrase. Moreover, the five-note chords share three pitch classes. The third phrase (m. 26) starts off related to the second as the second was to the first—its first dyad is the

second dyad in m. 24—but then continues past the span of the two previous statements. The result is a developmental process similar in some
ways to the beginning of Op.23 No. 2: the patterns of the first phrase
are preserved, but rearranged. In the Waltz many similar passages
demonstrate Schoenberg's growing ability to reconcile serial consistency and developing variation.

Other passages indicate Schoenberg's maturation in handling the
series. In mm. 14–15 the right hand plays a brief figure that starts out
as if it is a transposition of the opening motive of the composition (see

Ex. 4.20 Partitioning suggesting a transposition: mm. 1–4 and 13–15

Ex. 4.20). But, of course, it is not. What Schoenberg has found in his set
is that order positions 5, 7, and 8 are a transposition (T = 5) of order
positions 0–2 of the set. Thus, by partitioning the set in m. 14 so that
the B♭ (order position 6) is in a lower voice, and by assigning the
rhythm of m. 1 to order positions 5, 7, and 8, Schoenberg creates a
seeming transposition that breaks off from the continuation in m. 15
(E♭ instead of the transpositionally expected C which, however, does
appear in the left hand). Thus we have a typical, and eventually often
exploited, compositional subtlety here: on one hand this may be under-

stood as a varied transposition; on the other hand it should also be understood as the latter half of the set.

The Waltz marks off an important stage in the evolution of the serial idea. Schoenberg had now gathered enough experience with serial organization that he was able to use the series to provide both an underlying unity, as well as to guide the process of developing variation. Moreover, he felt confident enough of his skill in handling the series so that he could construct a movement of 113 measures based entirely on one set form.

Upon completing the Waltz, and with it Op.23, Schoenberg next turned his attention back to the Suite, Op.25 (19 February 1923). In doing so he transformed his earlier concept of this from a second series to *Klavierstücke* to a suite based on baroque models. After finishing the newly named Intermezzo in the style in which it had begun, he continued on to the next three movements, the Gavotte, Musette, and Menuet. These three movements were completed in a little more than a week, during which time he began the next two movements, the Trio and the Gigue, and also made brief sketches for a string quartet.[40] The Suite as a whole was finished by 8 March 1923.

The change from a set of *Klavierstücke* to a neo-Baroque suite was far more than a change of titles. In the other compositions Schoenberg interrupted over the years 1920–3, the earlier layer is never detectably different from the later.

Indeed, if the chronology were not known for these interrupted pieces (Op.23 No. 4, Op.25 Intermezzo, and so forth) no one would have thought to identify a difference between the earlier and later sections. This is so even though Schoenberg made substantial stylistic progress in the interim. Although the Intermezzo was completed without diverging from its earlier compositional premises, the 1923 movements of the Suite are markedly different from the Prelude and Intermezzo. Even though they are based on the same referential set, the 1923 movements deal with issues and organize the material in ways unthought of only two years earlier.

One of the clearest differences between the Gavotte and the movements begun in 1921 is the metric organization. In neither the Prelude nor the Intermezzo was there any substantive correspondence between the notated metre and the set structure. By contrast, in the Gavotte Schoenberg creates the 2/2, upbeat-to-downbeat metre, not merely by the placement of dynamics and durations but by the pitch organization as well. Although the solution for twelve-tone metre in this piece differs in some important respects from that of the mature twelve-tone style, the basis of the eventual solution can be traced back to this point.

---

[40] Transcribed in Maegaard, *Studien*, suppl., p. 60.

The opening measures of the Gavotte show the kinds of techniques employed to create the metre (see Ex. 4.21). By alternating between the right and left hands, with each figure one of the tetrachords of the set, Schoenberg sets up a regular pattern of repetition. A new tetrachord begins approximately every beat and closes on the following beat. Numerous other details support this basic metric pattern: the durations assigned, the placement of the first two accents, the common interval of closure for each right hand tetrachord (interval class 6) and each left hand tetrachord (interval class 1), but these are supportive details. The basis for the metric here is the referential pitch organization, the consistent recycling over half-measure spans of the three basic tetrachords of the set.

Schoenberg does not, of course, continue such regular patterns without interruption until the end of the work. Once the pattern has been

Etwas langsam (♩ = ca 72) nicht hastig

Ex. 4.21 Tetrachordally determined metre in the Gavotte, mm. 1–3

clearly established he begins, almost immediately, to play against it, forming a kind of metric dissonance, creating an implicit tendency to resolve with a return to metric regularity. Schoenberg employs just such a method to facilitate his move from the first to the second subject. After the metric regularity of mm. 1–3, the next pattern (mm. 4–5) is slightly extended (essentially, a written out ritard) and this is followed by two more forms that counter the previously established metre.

Beyond the metre, the other principal component of the neo-baroque character of the 1923 layer of Op.25 is the form. In the dance movements of the Suite Schoenberg employs those forms that were customarily used by Baroque-era composers of dance pieces: binary and rounded binary. However, these forms do not merely mimic the superficial motivic patterns of classical forms. Like the metre, the form is also based on set relationships—in this case on the choice and placement of set forms. The Menuett offers a good example of Schoenberg's procedures.

The form of the Menuett is a rounded binary (A = mm. 1–11; B = mm. 12–16; A′ = mm. 17–33). In the set tables, Schoenberg assigned labels to the forms. He called P-o 'T', R-o 'K', I-o 'DU', RI-o 'DuK', P-6 'D', R-6 'DeKr', I-6 'U', and RI-6 'KU'. It is very likely that the symbols 'T' and 'D' stand for tonic and dominant respectively.[41]

In a baroque binary form one of the means of articulating the 'B' section was by restating the opening motive transposed to the dominant. This confirms the harmonic motion of the 'A' section from the tonic to the dominant.

That is precisely the method Schoenberg uses here. He treats the set forms as a kind of analogy to chord progressions in the Baroque. The composition opens with P-o (the 'tonic') in mm. 1–2, progressing to I-6 (the inverted 'tonic') in mm. 3–4. The particular division of the tetra-chords—one per measure in the right hand, one tetrachord per two measures in the left hand—as well as the dotted rhythms appear only in these four measures in the 'A' section. This thematic idea, altered slightly, appears again immediately after the double bar. This time, the set forms are P-6 (the 'dominant') followed by I-o (the inverted 'dominant'). This is Schoenberg's serial analogy to the transposition of the motive to the dominant after the double bar in a baroque suite movement.

Similarly, the return to the 'A' section in m. 17 is marked not just by a return of the opening motivic material but, just as importantly, by the identical set progression: P-o followed by I-6.

By the standards of future pieces the relationship between form and set structure is rather elementary in the Menuett. There is nothing organic in these procedures—nothing really dependent on the specific structure of the set itself. Yet, however elementary such solutions were they are significant because they represent Schoenberg's first concerted attempts to relate set-form choice to form.[42] They are clear indications of Schoenberg's growing interest in making the set function on every level of the piece.

In the beginning of the discussion of the Suite evidence was cited, both from the set tables and the music, that supports a view of the 1921 layer of the Suite as based not on a serial linear ordering of the twelve pitch classes but, rather, on tritetrachordal polyphonic complex. This conception of the referential background of the piece is reinforced in the Gavotte, Musette, and Menuett. It would be impossible for anyone presented with only these movements to reconstruct a unique linear ordering. That picture changes completely in the last two movements written: the Trio and Gigue.

---

[41] That is the opinion of Brinkmann in Schoenberg, *Sämtliche Werke*, ser. B, iv. 77. This receives added support because the spelling of 'dominant' in German is '*Dominante*' and for R-6 Schoen-berg uses the label 'DeKr'. The symbols K and U stand for Krebs (retrograde) and Umkehrung (inversion) respectively.

[42] For a different reading of twelve-tone form in the Suite see Hyde, 'Musical Form', pp. 125–38.

In the Trio the set of this composition appears—for the first time—in linear orderings that relate to one another by the classical transformations of T, R, I, and RI. Schoenberg exploits this change of concept to articulate some of the properties of linearly ordered sets.

Up to this point, the normative subdivision of the set had been into its constituent tetrachords. In the Trio Schoenberg abandons the tetrachordal division of the set for a straightforward hexachordal division.

An immediate consequence of this subdivision is the emphasis of the harmonic equivalence of the two hexachords of the set. Both are pitchclass set 012346. This hexachord is one of the IH-combinatorial source hexachords, but Schoenberg is not using it to produce aggregates. Rather, the property that Schoenberg first exploits in his use of an IH-combinatorial hexachord is the harmonic equivalence of the two hexachords.

In the Gigue, as well, Schoenberg turned away from the tetrachordal division of the set, though the Gigue is not as regularly hexachordal as the Trio. Moreover, in the Gigue Schoenberg takes several significant steps forward in his stylistic development.

One of the problems that we know concerned Schoenberg in his early serial period was the worry that one set could not provide sufficient variety to be used as the exclusive basis of one composition. On aesthetic grounds, Schoenberg was on record as strongly opposed to literal repetitions in music and his fears of excessive set-induced repetitions must be seen in that light.[43]

In the serial compositions from this period Schoenberg experimented with a number of different solutions to this problem. He rotated the set in the Sonett, obscured the beginnings and endings of the set statements in the Waltz, or, as in many other compositions, simply abandoned the set to proceed with his development.

In the Gigue Schoenberg offers another solution. In m. 16 an ordering of the twelve tones occurs that cannot be derived directly from the referential twelve-tone set of the composition (see Ex. 4.22). There are clear developmental origins for this passage—the partitions of mm. 5–8 prepare the tritone successions—but this is a new ordering of the twelve tones for this composition.

In m. 19 another passage occurs that, once again, does not relate back to the referential ordering of the set. However, this passage is a serial transformation of m. 16. Similarly, passages in mm. 56, 71, and 72 are also serial transformations of m. 16.

Schoenberg has formed a subsidiary set and subjected it to the same kinds of serial transformations that are applied to the principal set.

---

[43] See for example Schoenberg's articles, 'New Music: My Music' and 'Criteria for the Evaluation of Music', in *Style and Idea*, pp. 102–4 and 129–31.

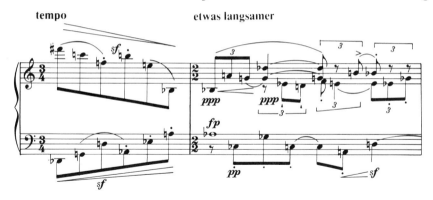

Ex. 4.22 Suite, Op. 25, Gigue, mm. 16–19: the subsidiary set in m. 16 and its serial transformation in m. 19

Although Schoenberg would later assert that a twelve-tone composition should be based on a single set, he did not hold to this limitation in the Suite, Op.25, nor, as we shall see, in other works of his early twelve-tone period. [44]

In the Gigue it is possible to see how thoroughly Schoenberg had consolidated the stylistic developments of the past few years. The set-determined formation of the metre, the refined use of isomorphic partitioning, the flexible, serially directed process of developing variation: these features are all found in this movement and are used with grace and skill.

After finishing the Suite, Op.25, on 8 March 1923, Schoenberg then turned his attentions back to the Serenade, now almost three years in gestation. Within eight days he completed the Variations and the Menuett and once again did not deviate perceptibly from the earlier compositional premises of these works. Then, he returned to the Sonett.

---

[44] Schoenberg's assertion can be found in 'Composition with Twelve Tones (1)', p.219.

At this point he changed the set to o t e 7 8 9 4 2 5 1 3 6, a reordering of the previous set: o t e 9 8 7 2 1 5 4 3 6. However, this reordering does not effect the kinds of structures he had sketched out the previous year. The rotation of the principal melody, the hierarchy of that line, and the idea of a multidimensional set presentation are all worked out here in full, as they had been sketched in the previous year.

Next, Schoenberg turned to the remaining movements of the Serenade, finishing them by 14 April 1923. The *Tanzscene*, left incomplete since August 1920, was taken up again on 30 March 1923 and finished a week later, in the style in which it had been begun three years earlier. The same day he resumed work on the *Tanzscene* Schoenberg also wrote the brief *Lied*. The last movement completed was the Finale. Neither of these last two movements is consistently serial and as such they represent an approach that was continually losing interest for Schoenberg. After this point, with a few exceptions, all of Schoenberg's compositions would be both serial and twelve-tone.

It is intriguing to speculate why after the conclusion of Opp.23–5 Schoenberg used only twelve-tone sets, never returning to the different-sized sets he used in these works. Perhaps there is no single answer, but the compositional procedures from this period suggest one possible explanation.

It appears as if Schoenberg had two principal concerns in the compositions from 1920–3: (1) solving the problems of serial ordering, i.e. learning how to make all events on the surface accountable to a referential ordering and (2) structuring his music to produce a regular circulation of the twelve tones.

As we have seen in this chapter, various solutions to these two problems emerged over the course of the years 1920–3. However, at some point, it apparently occurred to Schoenberg that the twelve-tone set—as opposed to sets with fewer, or more, tones—provided him with the opportunity to solve both of his problems simultaneously. That is, in his search for unity, we have seen Schoenberg, throughout the period in question, gradually move towards a surface in which more and more events are accountable to a referential serial ordering. At the same time, Schoenberg sought ways systematically to complete the chromatic. The twelve-tone set permitted him to accomplish both of these compositional aims simultaneously.

And, of course, as we shall see shortly, once Schoenberg started to use twelve-tone sets regularly, he immediately began to recognize some of the enormous compositional potential they presented, particularly when the sets were divided into harmonically equivalent hexachords, and even more so when he learned to make aggregates by combining different set forms, and still more so when he recognized the potential for hexachordal levels to articulate formal sections. Therefore, although he may have happened upon the twelve-tone set as a means of solving one set of compositional problems. Schoenberg had the musical sensitivity to recognize how other features could be transformed as well.

Looking back on the years 1920–3, one has to be impressed with the speed and power of Schoenberg's stylistic development. In these three years he moved from the most tentative experiments in serial thinking to quite successful compositional results. From a simple, almost ingenuous conception of serialism, he developed some important serial techniques: the permutation of elements, the reconciliation of developing variation and serial consistency, the formation of aggregates, the relationship of metre to set structure, the beginnings of hierarchical thinking and multidimensional set presentations. Perhaps the serial compositions from this period are tentative and elementary by later standards, but they demonstrate the extraordinary inventiveness of Schoenberg's compositional thinking, showing as they do a steady onward progression of learning and absorbing, challenging and discovering.

5

Ambitious Projects
The Wind Quintet, Op.26 and The Suite,
Op.29, 1923–1926

SCHOENBERG's experience with serial writing in the compositions Opp.23–5 left him poised and ready for more ambitious projects. He had developed enough skill in the use of his new method to be ready to tackle the problem of constructing large, abstract, forms—something he had not done since the String Quartet, Op.10, fifteen years earlier. A sense of his excitement and eagerness can be gathered from the chronology: on the very day he completed the Finale of the Serenade, Op.24 (14 April 1923), he also made the first sketches for the Wind Quintet, Op.26.[1] He gave every indication of a composer anxious to proceed with exciting ideas. And proceed he did. Over the next few months he worked at a fast pace on his new composition, finishing the first and second movements in May and July respectively, and setting down the beginnings of the third and fourth movements as well. But in the late summer of 1923 this intense activity came to an abrupt halt when Mathilde Schoenberg took ill. After her death in October of that year Schoenberg was unable to return to composition for some time and the Quintet was not finished until August 1924.

From a number of his published statements we know that Schoenberg was very concerned with the problem of atonal form. Moreover, he made it quite clear that he viewed the twelve-tone method as the answer to the formal problems posed by the abandonment of tonal harmony.

Schoenberg remarked:

Formerly the harmony had served not only as a source of beauty, but, more important, as a means of distinguishing the features of the form. For instance, only a consonance was considered suitable for an ending. Establishing functions demanded different successions of harmonies than roving functions; a bridge, a transition, demanded other successions than a codetta; harmonic variation could be executed intelligently and logically only with due consideration of the fundamental meaning of the harmonies.[2]

---

[1] The chronology of the works discussed in this chapter follows Jan Maegaard, *Studien, zur Entwicklung des dodekaphonen Satzes bei Arnold Schönberg*, 2 vols. and suppl. (Copenhagen, 1972), i. 115–20.

[2] 'Composition with Twelve Tones (1)', in *Style and Idea*, ed. Leonard Stein, trans. Leo Black (New York, 1975), 217.

He contrasted the clear structural functions of tonal harmony with the formal problems posed by his contextual music:

Fulfilment of all these functions—comparable to the effect of punctuation in the construction of sentences, of subdivison into paragraphs, and of fusion into chapters—could scarcely be assured with chords whose constructive values had not as yet been explored. Hence, it seemed at first impossible to compose pieces of complicated organization or of great length.[3]

During his contextual period he solved this problem by shaping the musical form in terms of the structure of a text:

A little later I discovered how to construct larger forms by following a text or a poem. The differences in size and shape of its parts and the change in character and mood were mirrored in the shape and size of the composition, in its dynamics and tempo, figuration and accentuation, instrumentation and orchestration. Thus the parts were differentiated as clearly as they had formerly been by the tonal and structural functions of harmony.[4]

But, clearly, this could not be a permanent solution for Schoenberg. He kept searching for a purely musical way to replace the structural functions of harmony:

After many unsuccessful attempts during a period of approximately twelve years, I laid the foundations for a new procedure in musical construction which seemed fitted to replace those structural differentiations provided formerly by tonal harmonies.

I called this procedure *Method of Composing with Twelve Tones Which are Related Only with One Another*.[5]

Schoenberg's description of his stylistic development is confirmed by his music. From the completion of his String Quartet No. 2 in 1908 until the beginnings of the serial period in 1920, he completed only three purely instrumental compositions: the *Klavierstücke*, Opp. 11 and 19, and the *Orchesterstücke*, Op. 16—each a collection of short movements. Every other composition from this period was set to a text.

At the beginning of the serial period, when Schoenberg was first learning how to manipulate the fundamental building-blocks of his new method, all of the compositions were relatively short movements. However, no sooner had he gained adequate experience than he began, at once, to construct the kinds of large, abstract forms that he had felt incapable of writing for fifteen years. The Wind Quintet is a large composition, lasting upwards of forty minutes in most performances. Moreover, some of the movements are exceptionally long and complex: the second movement alone is 419 measures.

Given the importance Schoenberg attached to the role of his new method in solving the problem of atonal form, it might seem somewhat

---

[3] Ibid., 217.   [4] Ibid., 217–18.   [5] Ibid., 218.

paradoxical that all of the movements are organized along traditional lines: the first movement is a sonata, the second a scherzo and trio, the third a song form, and the last a rondo. None the less, Schoenberg was not engaged in a superficial recycling of classical forms; he was not interested in mere thematic formalism. (Had he been, he could have written classical forms in his contextual period.) On the contrary, although they are cast in seemingly traditional moulds, the forms of the Wind Quintet are quite revolutionary. Here Schoenberg first experiments with making the structure of the twelve-tone set determine the shape and content of the form.[6] This is a remarkable step. It shows how quickly Schoenberg had internalized the twelve-tone system and how persistently he sought ways to make the structure of the set a compositional determinant, not just at the level of detail, but on all levels of musical structure.

In Schoenberg's earliest serial compositions, set-form choice was static: either a single form was used over and over (as in Op.23 No. 5, or the Sonett from Op.24) or a limited group of set forms was continuously recycled (as in Op.25). In none of these pieces were the formal subdivisions characterized by the choice of set forms. But, in Op.26, in an attempt to organize much larger spans of musical time, Schoenberg used the choice of set form to create the functional differentiation that distinguished the features of the form and determined the specific choice of those forms through the structure of the set.

The first movement begins with linear statements of P-0, R-0, and, I-0 in the flute (mm. 1–13). At the same time, the accompaniment consists entirely of partitioned statements of these set forms, as well as RI-0. Moreover, throughout the first twenty-three measures of the composition, only these four set forms are used.

What Schoenberg has done is to establish a referential collection of set forms. These four forms, by virtue of both temporal emphasis and their position at the beginning (and the end) of the composition, are treated as functionally similar to the tonic region in a tonal composition. In so doing Schoenberg has created a twelve-tone analogue for what he described as the 'establishing function'.

It should be recalled that hints of this idea have already appeared in *Die Jakobsleiter* where, at strategic points in the piece, the source hexachord returned at the original pitch level. However, the procedures of the Quintet are a clear step beyond that rudimentary idea. In *Die Jakobsleiter* the return to the original pitch level of the source hexachord

⁶ The role of set structure in the form of Op.26 is discussed in Andrew Mead, 'Large-Scale Strategy in Schoenberg's Twelve-Tone Music', *Perspectives of New Music*, 24 (1985), 131–40. See also his '"Tonal" Forms in Arnold Schoenberg's Twelve-Tone Music', *Music Theory Spectrum*, 9 (1987), 67–92.

affected but a single voice. Here, the referential region is established with the participation of all of the parts.

The specific choice of set forms for this opening region—P-o, I-o, and their retrogrades—is determined both on habitual and systematic grounds. In most of Schoenberg's serial compositions so far, and in most to come, I-o has been, and will remain, a commonly used counterpart of P-o. Even after Schoenberg turned to IH-combinatorially related combinations, and when, as a result, the polyphonic combination of P-o and I-o would no longer be possible, Schoenberg still persisted in using I-o as the counterpart of P-o—often making it the major component of a subsidiary area.

However, beyond these habitual grounds, the choice of I-o as the partner for P-o is based on the structure of this set. I-o holds invariant the content of the three disjunct tetrachords of P-o (see Ex. 5.1).

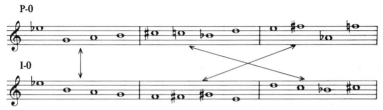

Ex. 5.1 Wind Quintet, Op. 26: invariant tetrachords, P-o and I-o

But Schoenberg was not interested in the direct use of this property: · the set is never divided into tetrachords and the tetrachordal invariance is never pointed out in a stark and simplistic manner. Rather, Schoenberg has much more subtle and interesting compositional aims.

Instead of merely asserting the equivalence of the tetrachords, Schoenberg exploits the common content of the discrete tetrachords for the purposes of developing variation. Normatively, the set is divided, not into tetrachords, but into hexachords. Each hexachord holds fixed four of the six pitch classes from each of the order corresponding hexachords in the I-related form (see Ex. 5.2).

The similar—but not identical—content of the hexachords allows Schoenberg to treat P-o and I-o as both inversions and variations of one another. For instance, the first hexachord of I-o (mm. 10–11)

Ex. 5.2 Common pitch-class content of the hexachords of P-o and I-o

should be understood as both a retrograde-inversion of the previous hexachord from R-0 (mm. 8–9) and a variation of its content. As we have seen, this was Schoenberg's solution to the problem of reconciling serial ordering and developing variation. It has now become a standard feature of Schoenberg's twelve-tone technique—really the first of the mature features to be perfected and employed on a regular basis.

Measure 29 initiates a transitional section which lasts until the entry of the second theme-group in m. 42. As Schoenberg remarked, a transition demands different kinds of successions than an establishing section. In the present case, the transition has its own particular content: P-0 and I-4. This is itself transitional, because the next section, the second theme-group, is characterized primarily by the set forms I-4 and I-9. Thus, the content of the transition (P-0 and I-4) marks an intermediate stage between the first theme-group (P-0 and I-0) and the second theme group (I-4 and I-9).

The formal procedures enacted here become the basis of the relationship between set-form choice and formal region in all of Schoenberg's twelve-tone compositions. Simply put, formal regions are characterized by, and delineated through, their set-form content. In the years to come Schoenberg would refine this idea, using IH-combinatorial four-groups to create regions characterized by the specific pitch-class content of the hexachords. Many other pieces of the puzzle would have to fall into place before those advanced procedures could be employed. (Although the set of Op.26 is IH-combinatorial, Schoenberg does not exploit that property in this piece, either to create aggregates or to determine hexachordal levels.)

Although not all of the mature features were completely worked out, none the less, the fundamental concepts of Schoenberg's twelve-tone form are present in Wind Quintet. From this point on, all of Schoenberg's larger twelve-tone compositions would delineate the opening section of the composition by means of a carefully limited, temporally stressed, group of set forms. These forms would establish a referential region. Subsidiary sections would be characterized by contrasting regions, whose content was determined by the structure of the set. Schoenberg used the stability of the opening referential region to create a structural dynamic: the move away from this referential region, creates formal instability, resolved only with the return of the referential group of set forms at the end of the movement, effecting closure. Although the details would be refined, the outlines of Schoenberg's mature solution are in place by this point.

The second theme-group, beginning at m. 42, is composed primarily of set forms I-4 and I-9. (Other forms do occur, receiving local emphasis, but I-4 and I-9 are the principal forms.) Schoenberg has relied on an important property of the set to determine the relationship between

Ex. 5.3 The set of the Wind Quintet, Op. 26, and the transpositional relationship between the hexachords

the set forms within this region: the second hexachord of the set is almost precisely a transposition of the first (see Ex. 5.3). Because of this property, the first hexachord of I-9 is almost identical to the second hexachord of I-4. This permits Schoenberg to create interesting developmental procedures on the local level. For instance, the flute in mm. 49–52 states the second hexachord of I-4. This is answered in the horn in mm. 51–3 by what at first seems to be a rhythmically free imitation (see Ex. 5.4). But, since this imitation is the first hexachord of I-9, and not the second of I-4, the final note of the figure in the horn is an E♭, not the F of the flute. Once again, Schoenberg has used the structure of the set to direct the developmental process.

Ex. 5.4 Wind Quintet, Op. 26, mm. 49–53: flute and horn

I-4 and I-9 were chosen as the principal components of the secondary area because of the invariant properties they hold with respect to P-0 (see Ex. 5.5). The invariant tetrachords, pentachords, and septachords permit this area to be understood as a logical outgrowth of earlier material. Because of their close relationship to P-0, melodic fragments from the second theme-group constantly recall phrases and ideas from earlier in the movement.

The recapitulation, beginning at m. 128, starts with a fairly straightforward repetition of the exposition. Of course, Schoenberg, as was his custom, did not repeat anything literally. Invariably, he made slight alterations in the rhythm, register, voicing, and dynamics. However, in general, the set-form succession is preserved: we have returned to the P-0/I-0 referential region.

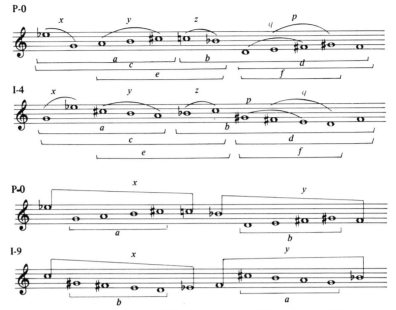

Ex. 5.5 Invariants held between P-0 and I-4; P-0 and I-9

The transition follows in m. 155. Continuing the analogy with tonal form, this transition does not simply repeat the transition from the exposition at its original pitch level, but transposes it (T = 5).

The choice of this interval for transposition is determined by the structure of the set. It is here that Schoenberg so clearly displays his interest in, and control of, the large-scale organization of the work, relating the form to the structure of the set.

The interval of transposition, coupled with both the structure of the set and the choice of set forms, ensures a powerful network of relationships. Compare, for instance, the second theme in the recapitulation with the equivalent spot in the exposition (see Ex. 5.6).

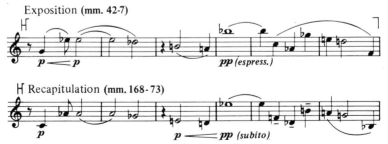

Ex. 5.6 A comparison of the second theme in the recapitulation with the second theme in the exposition

Since these two set forms are T-5 related, it follows that the second hexachord of one will be virtually identical to the first of the other. Such is the case with every comparable passage. Therefore, the latter half of the recapitulation is both a transposition and, at the same time, a varied repetition of the second half of the exposition. Schoenberg accomplished this, not by *ad hoc* developmental procedures but by using the structure of the set to determine his choice of set forms.

Moreover, since I-4 and I-9 were used as the principal set forms for the second theme group in the exposition, the T-5 relationship means that I-9 remains invariant as a component of the second theme in the recapitulation.

The formal structure of the first movement of the Wind Quintet offers compelling evidence of Schoenberg's unceasing efforts to exploit the potential of the twelve-tone system. From the beginning of his serial period he has been learning, step by step, how to structure every aspect of his music in terms of the new method. As soon as he gained the requisite experience and control over local relationships he attempted to solve the problem of form. The solution of Op. 26 would be refined over the next few years, but the fundamental principles had been laid down: sections are characterized by their set-form content; the specific content is determined by the structure of the set.

Although the Wind Quintet represents a significant step forward in the formal realm, other procedures reveal Schoenberg at a more elementary stage in his development.

One of the earliest issues Schoenberg faced as a serial composer was the problem of constructing a polyphonic fabric from a referential *linear* idea. This would prove to be a difficult problem and it would trouble Schoenberg throughout his early serial period.

In the earliest serial compositions Schoenberg tended to solve this in one of two ways: (1) He would layer set statements in different voices. Thus, a three-voice polyphonic fabric would require three set forms, a four-voice fabric, four, and so forth. (2) He would divide the set into segments and state the segments as chords.

These two basic solutions could be varied in a number of ways. For instance, instead of presenting complete linear statements in each voice, Schoenberg might divide the set into hexachords, with the hexachords stated as lines (see the first movement, mm. 20–1). Or the two methods might be combined. One line might state the set as a line in one voice, accompanied by other set forms, divided into chords (see the second movement, mm. 1–6).

These two methods permitted Schoenberg to create a polyphonic fabric with every note relating back to a single referential set. However, these solutions also created serious compositional problems—problems that would trouble Schoenberg for the next few years.

The most obvious of these is melodic. If, as is so often the case, each of the different voices is a linear representation of the set, then that particular melodic pattern will appear quite frequently. If the composition is long, this can lead to real problems of melodic variety, for the same linear patterns are repeated over and over.

That is the dilemma Schoenberg faced in this work. He was committed to using the set as the referential basis of the entire composition. Yet, his methods of generating polyphony led directly to the overuse of a limited group of linear ideas. He was thus forced to find some way to expand the repertoire of available melodic patterns, without violating his commitment to serial consistency.

Schoenberg solved this problem by employing the operation of rotation. For example, the theme of the second movement, stated first in the oboe in mm. 1–7, is a rotation of P-0. It begins with order position 3, continues through the final order position and concludes with order positions 0 1 2 (see Ex. 5.7).

By means of the operation of rotation, Schoenberg was able to generate new melodic material that was clearly derived from and related to the referential set, yet sufficiently different that it solved, at least provisionally, the problem of melodic variety.[7]

Rotation was not a permanent solution, nor a very subtle one. It remained an active part of Schoenberg's vocabulary only for a short time. As he developed other techniques—particularly partitioning—rotation became less necessary for melodic variety. Moreover, it ceased to be a viable option after aggregate forming IH-combinatoriality became a regular feature of Schoenberg's method. For not only could rotation work counter to aggregate formation but it could also create hexachords other than those found in the IH-combinatorial set complex, and thus upset the role hexachordal levels played in formal differentiation.

Schoenberg's two methods of generating polyphony created other problems as well. These may be described as a paradox: if the set is stated as chords, then how do the resultant lines relate to the orginal set? But, if lines are formed by linear statements of the set, then how are the other voices generated, and how do the simultaneities relate to the referential set?[8]

---

[7] Schoenberg indicated that the use of rotation technique originated in the need for melodic variety. See 'Composition with Twelve Tones (1)', pp. 229–30. As Schoenberg remarked: 'The production of such variants is not only necessary in larger forms, especially in Rondos, but useful also in smaller structures.' However, this technique was 'necessary' only in the early serial period, where there was a reliance on linear set presentations. This procedure is not a feature of the mature twelve-tone compositions.

[8] This problem is given a thorough discussion in Peter Westergaard, 'Toward a Twelve-Tone Polyphony', *Perspectives of New Music*, 4 (1966), 90–112.

Ex. 5.7 Rotation: the theme of the second movement, mm. 1–11

The Quintet is troubled throughout by this paradox. Where Schoenberg states the set as a succession of chords, the resultant lines often seem to have only local significance. Where the polyphony is created by layered set statements, the harmonies lack focus. Two examples should help to illustrate this (see Ex. 5.7 above and Ex. 5.8).

In mm. 1–6 (Ex. 5.7), P-0 is divided into trichords and stated, more or less homophonically, in the clarinet, horn, and bassoon. Clearly, the simultaneities relate to, and are derived from, the referential set.

But what is the function of the clarinet line, G B B♭ G♭ (mm. 1–8)? This line is formed from order positions 1 3 6 9. Yet, it is not harmonically equivalent to any of the embedded segments of the set. Nor does it represent a group of pitch classes prominent as a collection in any of the

Ex. 5.8 Second movement, mm. 111–16

important set forms used in the piece (I-o, I-4, I-9). Nor does this particular pattern recur with any degree of consistency in the remainder of
the movement.

Conversely, in Ex. 5.8, the individual lines are all linear statements of
the set. But what role do the simultaneities play? No consistent harmonies of any sort emerge; the rate of change is too fast. Nor are there
recurrent intervallic patterns. In short, these relationships appear to
have only local significance.[9]

[9] A similar view of Schoenberg's local harmonic relationships can be found in Arnold Whittal,
Schoenberg Chamber Music (Seattle, 1972), 41–2. This is not to say that Op. 26 lacks musically interesting harmonic relationsips. See Mead, '"Tonal" Forms, p. 178.

Throughout the Quintet Schoenberg came up against this paradox: if he made the lines conform to the set, then the simultaneities lacked focus, but if he formed the simultaneities from segments of the set, then the lines lacked direction. This would remain a persistent and perplexing problem during this period.

However, the seeds of the solution are found in some interesting compositional procedures in the third movement, though, clearly, Schoenberg did not realize their full implications at this point.

The third movement opens with a duet between the horn and bassoon (see Ex. 5.9). Three statements of P-0 occur here, partitioned between the two instruments. Each order position of P-0 is represented in the horn line: 0 5 6 e from the first statement, 1 4 7 t from the second, 2 3 8 9 from the last. (This partitioning is anticipated in the first movement. See mm. 94, 98–100, and elsewhere. The 056e extraction was important for pointing out the similarities between P-0 and I-9.)

Thus, the horn creates a new twelve-tone set and throughout the movement it appears frequently. (Schoenberg even made up a limited table for this subsidiary set).[10]

The motivation for creating this new set was probably quite mundane: having used rotation extensively in the second movement, Schoenberg felt the need for even more melodic material to provide variety. The extraction of a new twelve-tone set from the original set must have seemed like a plausible option.

But what started out so prosaically would eventually become a corner-stone of the mature style, for, although the compositional implications would not be realized for some time, a number of the most advanced characteristics of the mature style can be traced back to this passage.

This two-dimensional thinking would eventually lead to the solution for Schoenberg's problems of melodic variety and harmonic consistency. With this kind of partitioning he could generate new melodic ideas by extracting elements from a succession of local set statements. Therefore, the melodic content would no longer have to be tied to strict linearizations of the set. At the same time local, vertical relationships could be formed from segments of the set itself.

Moreover, the unfolding of an aggregate over several local set statements would become one of the central features of the mature style. By creating a middleground aggregate that subsumes other, local aggregates, Schoenberg established different hierarchical levels.

However, we must remember that at this stage Schoenberg had not yet systematized a generalized notion of the aggregate as something distinct from the twelve-tone set. The concept of chromatic completion

---

[10] A facsimile of these tables is reprinted in Martha Hyde, 'The Format and Function of Schoenberg's Twelve-Tone Sketches', *Journal of the American Musicological Society*, 36 (1983), 456.

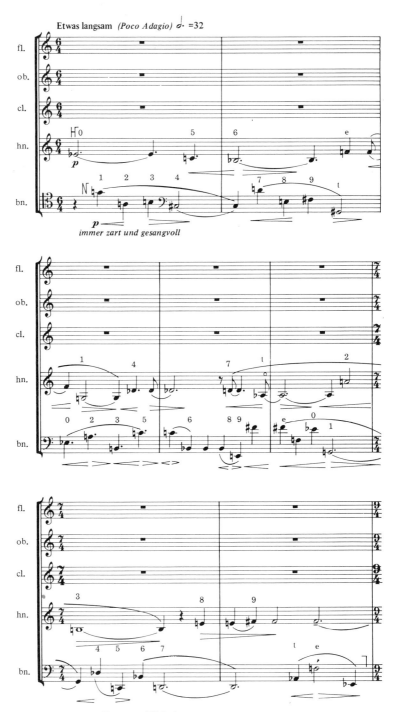

Ex. 5.9 Third movement, mm. 1–7

had led to the twelve-tone set, but up to this point Schoenberg had not yet developed the later refinement that segments of twelve-tone set forms could be systematically combined to create aggregates. The extracted twelve-tone set may have originated as a means of generating more melodic material, but the procedures Schoenberg learned here would eventually have far-reaching consequences.

The pattern of extraction from the original set is very interesting. From each of the three local set statements Schoenberg extracts four notes. Each of those four-note units symmetrically divides the set. The first group takes order postions o 5 6 e from P-o: that is, the first and last order positions of each hexachord. Similarly, the second group extracts order positions 1 4 7 t: the second and fifth notes of each hexachord. The final tetrachord, order positions 2 3 8 9, extracts the third and fourth notes of each hexachord.

Moreover, the extracted set has some interesting properties. The first and third extracted tetrachords are pitch-class set 0257; the middle tetrachord pitch-class set 0167. Since the first and third are T-6 related, and since the middle tetrachord maps into itself under this transposition, it follows that at T-6 the content of the three tetrachords is preserved. Schoenberg uses this property to determine the choice of transposition within the movement.

In mm. 53–60 three rotated statements of R-6 occur, partitioned according to the order-number scheme of Ex. 5.9 with the extracted twelve-tone set in the flute. Thus, given the properties described above, the tetrachords of this passage are identical to those of the opening measures of the movement.

Here again is unmistakable evidence of Schoenberg's greatest accomplishment from this period: the specific level of transposition is determined by the structure of the set—in this case the subsidiary set. Schoenberg was learning how to make the structure of the set determine an impressive array of compositional features.

The logic of the third movement's partitioning scheme, its relationship to events in the first movement, and its impact on the form of the movement might lead one to suspect that it could have been Schoenberg's initial idea for the movement. It might suggest that Schoenberg—as he did in so many other pieces—sketched out an initial idea that was filled with possibilities, and then proceeded to realize them. Nothing could be further from the case. An examination of Schoenberg's sketches for this movement offers us a tantalizing glimpse into Schoenberg's compositional process and gives us some hint of his tremendous excitement as he searched for solutions to the problems posed by his material.

Schoenberg began work on the Quintet on 14 April 1923. Over the next two weeks he worked out mm. 1–47 of the first movement. Then,

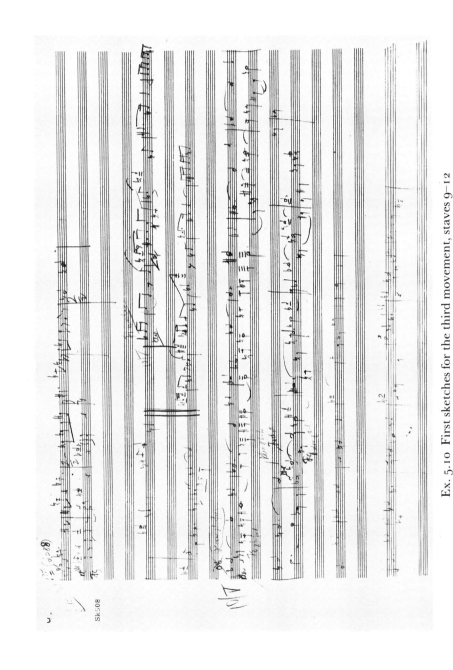

Ex. 5.10 First sketches for the third movement, staves 9–12

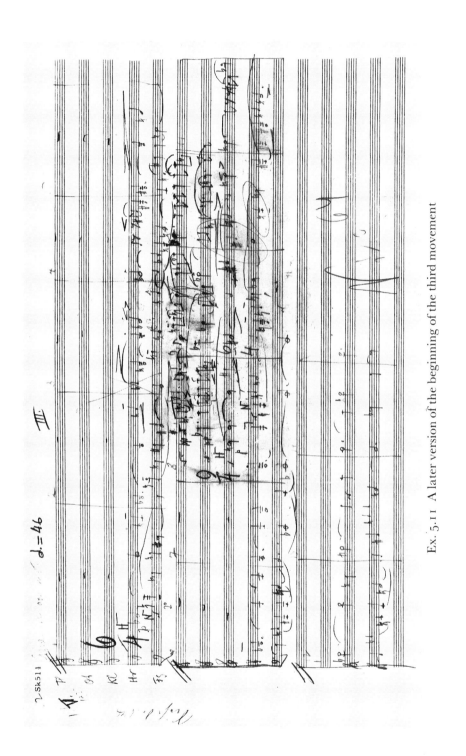

Ex. 5.11 A later version of the beginning of the third movement

on 10 May 1923, he sketched out ideas for the remaining three movements (see Ex. 5.10). The sketches for the second movement occupy the
first two staves; staves 5 and 6 (right side) present the last movement's
theme. On staves 9–12 Schoenberg sketched out a passage that very
closely resembles the beginning of the third movement.

However, the differences between this sketch and the final version
are far more than cosmetic: absolutely none of the properties characteristic of the final version is in the first sketch. The upper voice does not
unfold a new twelve-tone set: over the three statements of P-0, thirteen
notes appear in the top line, but both E and B are missing. There is no
symmetrical extraction from the hexachords, no equivalence of the first
and last tetrachord. In fine, all of the properties that permitted Schoenberg to construct a middleground set presentation, to relate it to passages in the first movement, to use its properties to determine the
transpositional levels of the form—all these properties are absent. We
are left then with an extracted melody that seems to have little more
than local function.

Five days later Schoenberg returned to this movement. He reworked
the opening measures, this time with the instrumentation and rhythm
virtually the same as the final version (see Ex. 5.11). But still he per-

Ex. 5.12 Schoenberg's discovery of the subsidiary set

sisted with the extracted melody of the earlier sketch. However, in this sketch is the first sign that something was troubling him.

At some point, Schoenberg looked back over his sketch, and noticed that not only was E♭ the first note of the extracted line, but that also it reappeared just four notes later. Clearly he did not yet have a formalized plan to create a new twelve-tone set in this voice, but this early repetition must have seemed inappropriate, so he crossed out the note.

The next sketch is dated 1 June 1923 (see Ex. 5.12). Schoenberg immediately started to solve the problem of the too early repetition of the E♭. He began another sketch of the opening measures. This time the repeated E♭ is conspicuously absent. Schoenberg worked his way through two statements of P-0, extracting nine notes in the upper voice (see staves 7–8, Ex. 5.12).

Suddenly, before the completion of the third statement of P-0, the sketch breaks off.

Immediately below, Schoenberg starts again, sketching out a new opening for the movement, this time the final version. Clearly, Schoenberg had come upon the idea of the extracted twelve-tone set, and had begun to see some of the many compositional possibilities that it offered. A mark of his pleasure can be seen at the bottom of the page, where he drew a diagram which represents his partitioning scheme, and next to it a note, meant as much for future scholars as for himself: 'I believe Goethe would be quite satisfied with me.'[11]

Nothing could more graphically illustrate Schoenberg's joy of discovery, his process of self-criticism, his constant searching for solutions, than this sequence of sketches. We are treated to a rare glimpse of the birth of an idea. Here, before our eyes, we see Schoenberg wrestling with a problem, and in solving it finding the key to enter a new world of compositional possibilities. In Schoenberg's long odyssey, the compositional discoveries of the third movement of the Quintet mark one of the more decisive stages.

In October 1924, only two months after concluding the Wind Quintet, Schoenberg began work on the Suite, Op.29. At that time he made a number of preliminary sketches and worked out a few passages, at first for an ensemble without piano. Serious work began several months later; between June and August of 1925 Schoenberg completed the second and third movements, mm. 1–136 of the first movement, and the beginning twenty-two measures of the last movement. Then, as so often in his career, he interrupted his work, this time to write Opp.27

---

[11] In the first issue of the *Journal of the Arnold Schoenberg Institute*, the editor, Leonard Stein, raised the issue of the meaning of Schoenberg's diagram and its accompanying cryptic remark. See *Journal of the Arnold Schoenberg Institute*, 1 (1976), 5. In a later issue, a number of solutions were suggested by readers: ibid., 1 (1977), 181–90. Although the meaning of Schoenberg's diagram was clarified, the specific intention of his mention of Goethe ('Ich glaube Goethe müsste ganz zufrieden mit mir sein') is far less certain.

and 28. Schoenberg did not return to the Suite, Op.29, until April 1926, completing the work the following month. Although the composition bears a later opus number than the choral works of Opp.27 and 28, most of it was written a year before those compositions. Thus, the Suite represents an earlier stage of Schoenberg's development than the choral works, and is properly treated here.

One of the most impressive characteristics of Schoenberg's compositional development is the painstaking care with which he refined his method. Every composition introduces new problems and proposes new solutions, but in a carefully controlled process.

Nowhere is that more apparent than in the Suite, Op.29. The great accomplishments of the first serial compositions–the reconciliation of serial order and developing variation, the exploitation of invariants, the refined use of isomorphic partitioning—all of these are now permanent features of Schoenberg's style. Furthermore, the procedures of the Wind Quintet—including the interaction of set structure and form—are continued, and polished in the Suite. Moreover, having solved some old problems Schoenberg was free to turn his attention to some new issues.

We have seen in the Wind Quintet that no sooner had Schoenberg developed sufficient skills, he immediately confronted—squarely, and without hesitation—the problem of large-scale form. One of the central accomplishments of the Wind Quintet was the relationship between form and the structure of the set. The Suite, Op.29, demonstrates that those achievements were not isolated experiments: in this work as well, the form is intimately tied to the structure of the set. Once again, though seemingly cast in neoclassic moulds, the forms of the Suite are not superficial recyclings of anachronistic thematic patterns. Rather, Schoenberg continued to develop an autonomous concept of twelve-tone form in which the content of the form is determined by the structure of the set.

This is particularly evident in the first movement, the Ouverture. The movement is a large binary structure, with the second principal section (the 'recapitulation', mm.131–230) a modified repetition of the first (the 'exposition', mm. 1–130). Each of these two larger sections is subdivided into two principal subdivisions. In the exposition, following a brief introduction (mm. 1–3), the first theme-group lasts through m. 67; it is followed by a Ländler (mm. 68–130). The recapitulation is anything but literal: the first theme-group is freely reordered; the Ländler is greatly abbreviated.

Just as in the Wind Quintet, Schoenberg establishes a group of set forms at the beginning of the composition that are treated as a referential complex. In the Suite this referential group of forms includes P-0, I-0, I-5, I-7, and their retrogrades. They are, with minor exceptions, the only set forms used in the first twenty-eight measures of the movement.

The first half of the exposition is subdivided into three subsections (mm. 1–28, 29–49, 50–67), the last of which is a variant of the first. This miniature ternary form, embedded within the large framework of the movement, contains a small-scale version of twelve-tone form: the first subsection contains only the referential collection of set forms; the second moves away to other areas; the third brings us back to the referential collection where it closes.

In the recapitulation this plan is preserved, somewhat loosely, in retrograde: the two outer subsections switch position, while the middle subsection remains in place. As a result, this half of the recapitulation mimics the formal plan of the exposition, including its initial delineation of the referential group of set forms and the final return to that group.

Although the outer subsections of the ternary form are repeated—however altered—at their original pitch level in the recapitulation, that is not the case for the middle section. Measures 29–49 of the exposition reappear in the recapitulation at mm. 141–61 in inversion.

With some minor exceptions Schoenberg consistently replaces any given set form from the middle subsection of the exposition with its index number 11 (IN-e)-related equivalent in the recapitulation.[12] Thus, I-1 in the exposition reappears as P-t in the recapitulation (mm. 29–32 vs. 141–4), R-t returns as RI-1 (mm. 33–6 vs. 145–8), and so forth.

In the Wind Quintet the specific choice of transposition for the recapitulation was determined by the structure of the set. The same holds for the choice of IN-e in the recapitulation of the Suite.

The set of the Suite is 0 4 3 7 e 8 9 6 5 1 2 t. The disjunct hexachords are third-order all-combinatorial: pitch-class set 014589. This hexachord excludes three intervals: 2, 6, and t. As a result, the forty-eight set forms are divided into two disjunct groups of twenty-four forms each: one group has hexachords with the pitch content C Eb E G G♯ B and C♯ D F F♯ A Bb; the other, hexachords C C♯ E F G♯ A and D Eb F♯ G Bb B.

The choice of IN-e for the recapitulation is determined by these properties. Any pair of IN-e-related forms of this set have hexachords with the same pitch-class content. Thus, for example, I-1 has the same hexachords as P-t, P-6 the same as I-5, and so forth. Therefore, since every set form from the exposition is replaced by its IN-e counterpart in the recapitulation, it follows that the content of the disjunct hexachords will be preserved. This means that, at one and the same time, set forms

[12] Index number is described in Milton Babbitt, 'Twelve-Tone Rhythmic Structure and the Electronic Medium', *Perspectives of New Music*, 1 (1962), 57.

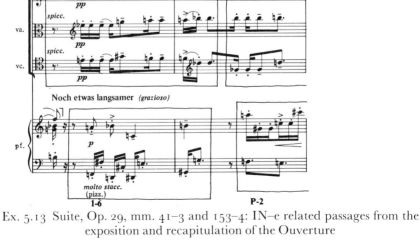

Ex. 5.13 Suite, Op. 29, mm. 41–3 and 153–4: IN–e related passages from the exposition and recapitulation of the Ouverture

from the recapitulation can be understood as both inversions and as reorderings of their counterparts from the exposition (see Ex. 5.13).

As in the Wind Quintet, Schoenberg has structured his form around the properties of his set. The formal plan of the Ouverture does not work with every set, nor at every index number. Rather, Schoenberg has looked into the structure of the set and found a property, particular to that set, that permits him to make the set a compositional determinant on the largest scale of musical structure.

The last part of the exposition, the Ländler, is much altered and abbreviated when it returns in the recapitulation. Here too, Schoenberg devises a plan for large-scale coherence.

The Suite as a whole is one of Schoenberg's most playful compositions, filled with light-hearted references to popular and folk music. The Ländler offers a particularly clear example of this, as it begins with a stuttering 'oom-pah' and a 'tonic-to-dominant' bass (see Ex. 5.14).

The D-A bass of mm. 68–79 is followed, over the course of this section, by a succession of transpositions: B♭-F, G-D, and A-E. What is of interest formally, is the lack of a stable dyad or collection. The constant changes in the transpositional level preclude any perception of structural stability or consistency. Even the temporal emphasis on D-A is contradicted, at the end of this section, by closing with an A-E bass. Absent as well is any referential collection of set forms: neither the collection established in the first part of the exposition (P-0, I-0, I-5, and I-7), nor any other stable collection of set forms, holds sway.

This structural instability is resolved in the recapitulation. There, the Ländler—much abbreviated—begins with the bass dyad B–F♯. This dyad receives a certain degree of temporal emphasis (mm. 202–9). Then, quickly, Schoenberg moves through D–G (mm. 210–11), B♭–E♭ (mm. 212–13), and finally back to B–F♯ (see Ex. 5.15).

Schoenberg has applied the same transposition interval, T-4, three times in succession to the bass dyad. Thus, after the third transposition he cycles back to the original dyad, B–F♯, effecting a simple kind of closure.

However, beyond this rudimentary notion of closure lies something far more significant. The reapplication of T-4 to a dyad of interval class 5 creates the hexachord, pitch-class set 014589. This is, of course, the hexachord of the set of the Suite. Moreover, not only is this the hexachord of the set but, also, it is at the same pitch level as the three principal referential set forms of the composition (P-0, I-5, I-7).

In Schoenberg's earliest serial compositions, linear continuity was formed by, and comprised of, linearized segments of the set. We have seen some of the problems this caused: in particular, melodic repetitiveness. In the Wind Quintet, in an attempt to counter these problems, Schoenberg developed the technique of rotation and also constructed a

Ex. 5.14 Suite, Op. 29, first movement, mm. 68–78: the opening of the
Ländler

subsidiary set. The hexachord, unfolded over the Ländler, represents
another approach to this problem, one that would become a central
feature of Schoenberg's method.

Schoenberg has conjoined elements of a number of different set forms
to produce a line that cuts across local set statements. This is of central
importance because in so doing he creates a middleground level of
structure, one in which the notes have multiple function—both locally,
within the individual set statements, and over a longer span as well.

But even beyond this is something else of paramount interest—the

(continued)

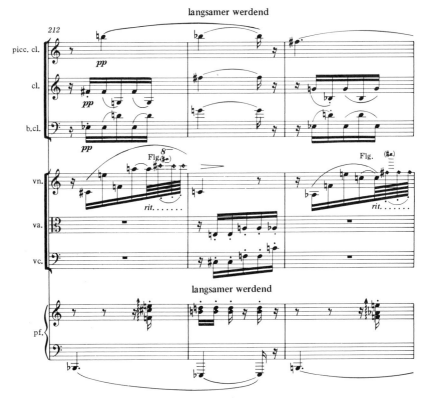

Ex. 5.15 Suite, Op. 29, first movement, mm. 202–14: the abbreviated
Ländler

growing intersection and interrelationship of the different compositional domains. In the Ländler, the 'tonic-dominant' bass is formed by
extracting order positions 0 and 3 (e and 8 from R-forms). Thus, the
unfolding middleground hexachord is a result of a union between local
set choice, partitioning, and set structure.

In the Suite, the creation of middleground structures is not limited to
the *Ländler*. Rather, throughout the work, in a number of different contexts, Schoenberg demonstrates his increasing concern for issues of hierarchy, and realizes this through the formation of numerous structures
that transcend individual, local set statements. This interest can be seen
in a variety of contexts, with a remarkable diversity of method.

A familiar approach to this problem can be found in the second
movement, the *Tanzschritte*, the first movement written. In mm. 15–21,
as in the third movement of the Quintet, Schoenberg creates a middleground melodic structure by extracting elements from a succession of
local set statements. This subsidiary set unfolds in the violin part.

The similarities with the third movement of the Quintet are unmistakable: the subsidiary set is formed by extracting four notes each of three local set statements. As in the Quintet, here too, Schoenberg creates a symmetrical order-number pattern. In this case he extracts order positions 0369 from the first set statement, t741 from the second, and 258e from the third. Moreover, here, as in the Quintet, each of the extracted segments is hexachordally isomorphic.

Moreover, beyond the common points of intersection with Op.26, Schoenberg experiments with a new feature, one that bears careful attention. The partitions yield the following order-number tetrachords: 0369, 147t, 258e. Because of the fixed order-number interval (3) these three tetrachords are related to one another and can be derived from one another.[13] Thus, for example, 147t can be derived from 0369 by the addition of a constant (1). What Schoenberg has done is to transfer the operations of the pitch domain to the rhythmic domain: this is transposition of order numbers. Clearly, Schoenberg was starting to exploit the characteristics of the twelve-tone system in ways that were truly revolutionary.

The third movement provides another example of Schoenberg's increasing concern with issues of hierarchy. This movement, a set of variations on the tune 'Ännchen von Tharau', marks another important stage in Schoenberg's development. Here Schoenberg returns to the problem of multidimensional set statements. Fitting a tonal theme into a twelve-tone composition may seem somewhat anomalous, and so it is. But Schoenberg is not serious: this is but one of many playful, or tongue-in-cheek references in this composition. It should not prevent us from recognizing the serious accomplishments of this movement.

It should be recalled that in the Sonett Schoenberg generated his melodic line by the *ad hoc* extraction of several notes from each local set statement. This created a primitive multidimensional fabric in which both the accompaniment, and the unfolding melodic line were derived from the same referential background. In these Variations Schoenberg returns to the multidimensional idea. However, here, a mere three years later than the Sonett, we can see the profound effect of his intervening experience.

The opening of the first variation offers a clear example of the dis-

---

[13] These order-number tetrachords are related to one another and derivable from one another only by virtue of order position, not through interval content. Perhaps the musical usefulness of this partitioning is less than the related partitioning in Op.26 precisely because of the lack of invariant interval-class relationships. In Op.26, it will be recalled, the partitioned tetrachords remain invariant under T-6, a relationship that Schoenberg exploited to structure the form of that movement. No such invariant relationships are present here. Resonances of the idea of transferring operations from one domain to another have clear consequences in contemporary theory and compositional practice. See for example ibid. Also, John Rahn, 'On Pitch or Rhythm: Interpretations of Ordering of and in Pitch and Time', *Perspectives of New Music*, 13 (1975), 182–203.

tance Schoenberg had travelled since the multidimensional set presentations of the Sonett (see Ex. 5.16). The theme appears in the cello, alternating between the second and first note of each measure. Each note of the evolving melody is supported by, and is part of, a local set statement. Unlike the Sonett, where there was no set-form choice, here the choice of each local set form is determined by two carefully defined constraints: (1) Schoenberg establishes a regular alternation of P- and I-forms. This is a compositional decision of paramount importance, for it is by this alternation that he preserves the hierarchical priority of the slowly evolving theme. (2) Isomorphic partitioning is applied to each of

Ex. 5.16 Suite, Op. 29, third movement mm. 23–32: the beginning of the first variation

the local set statements. The melody notes are alternately assigned order positions o and 1 (e and t in the R-forms). Coupled with the regular alternation of P- and I-forms this means that all P-forms have the melody note in order position o, while the I-forms place it in order position 1.

The regular alternation of P- and I-forms, coupled with the isomorphic partitioning, means that the choice of local set forms is virtually predetermined. Given the first set form (I-o), it follows that for the next melody note (Db) a form must be chosen that places Db in order position o. This must be either a P- or an R-form. There are only two such forms, and given the peculiar characteristics of Schoenberg's set, they are almost identical. Schoenberg chose P-t. Similarly, the generation of the remaining local set forms is determined by the course of the melody, coupled with the alternation of P- and I-forms, with a fixed partitioning.

Similar multidimensional set presentations appear in the other variations as well. With this movement Schoenberg has developed most of the more important characteristics of his mature multidimensional set presentations. Although the context for this momentous achievement is a seemingly frivolous movement, with its odd mixture of tonal and atonal elements, this should not distract us from recognizing the importance of Schoenberg's accomlishment. He has created a clear hierarchy, with the slowly unfolding melody generated by the conjunction of elements of a succession of local set forms.

In other dimensions as well, the Suite, Op.29, represents a decided advance in Schoenberg's technical evolution, particularly in his handling of combinatoriality and the aggregate.

In the Suite Schoenberg continues to discover and exploit more of the properties of combinatoriality. His previous twelve-tone compositions—the Waltz from Op.23, the Sonett from Op.24, the Suite, Op.25, and the Quintet, Op.26—all used sets that were combinatorial. Yet, in none of those compositions was the property exploited as it would be in the mature twelve-tone compositions: both the Waltz and the Sonett use but one set form apiece; the set of Op.25 is either divided into tetrachords or, when it is divided into hexachords, is not combined with its IH-combinatorial partner; the set of Op.26 is often divided into hexachords but, with one exception, IH-combinatorially related set forms are never combined.

The Suite, Op.29, with its all-combinatorial set, makes a perceptible step towards the systematic exploitation of combinatoriality. In numerous passages in the composition Schoenberg states combinatorially related set forms opposite one another and in the process creates aggregates.

However, although Schoenberg does exploit combinatoriality to a limited degree, he is still far from the mature style. In the mature compositions, IH-combinatoriality was the norm of local set-association, combination, and succession. Invariably, in those works, if a set form is to be combined polyphonically with another form, it will be combined only with its IH-combinatorial counterpart. Moreover, local regions were established primarily by the presence of IH-combinatorial set complexes.

Nothing like that consistency is present in the Suite, Op.29. In spite of the all-combinatorial structure of the set, there are relatively few instances where two set forms are combined or juxtaposed so as to form aggregates. More often, Schoenberg's manipulation of the surface prevents any aggregate formation: either he combines non-combinatorially related set forms, layers multiple set forms on top of one another, avoids lining up the corresponding hexachords, divides the set into tetrachords, and so forth. In sum, hexachordal combinatoriality is an isolated procedure in the Suite, and therefore has none of the profound implications of the later works: there is no impact on the form, no control of the harmony, no systematic creation of aggregates.

Similarly, although the Suite shows development in the formation of aggregates, none the less, this idea is at a relatively elementary stage. Since Schoenberg does not use IH-combinatoriality in a systematic manner, aggregates are not yet treated as fundamental units of progression. In the mature works, where the time line can often be divided into a succession of aggregates, where aggregates are formed by combining IH-combinatorially related sets, and where middleground aggregates occur frequently, aggregates literally saturate the surface, often in several dimensions. That is hardly the case in the Suite, Op.29.

However, a number of signs point to the gathering importance of this idea. Many passages in the Suite are clearly formulated so as to create aggregates. In the process Schoenberg developed some of the techniques that would eventually permit him to create a fabric in which aggregates could permeate the surface.

The Wind Quintet, Op.26, and the Suite, Op.29, represent a major turning-point in Schoenberg's twelve-tone development. It is here that Schoenberg first satisfactorily resolved a crucial issue: Can the twelve-tone method be used to solve the problems of atonal form? The answer was a resounding yes, for in these two compositions Schoenberg learned how to make the structure of the set participate at all levels of the form-building process. That is not the only accomplishment: in these two compositions Schoenberg also made major advances in his treatment of invariance, combinatoriality, and the aggregate. None the less, Schoenberg's treatment of twelve-tone form remains the major success of this period, a testament to the scope and courage of his vision.

6

Further Refinements

The Choral Pieces, Opp. 27 and 28, 1925

IN September 1925 Schoenberg interrupted his work on the nearly complete Suite, Op. 29, and began to compose a series of choral works: the Four Pieces for Mixed Choir, Op. 27, and the Three Satires, Op. 28. These compositions occupied his attention until December 1925, a four-month interlude in the middle of his work on the Suite.[1]

Six of the seven compositions are twelve-tone. Each is based on its own set—posing and solving a series of related compositional problems. Each of the two collections contains several short a cappella works and each, as well, has one relatively large composition for chorus with the accompaniment of an instrumental ensemble.

Although these may not be Schoenberg's most ambitious compositions, they are of more than a little importance in the chronology of his evolving twelve-tone syntax. Coming, as they do, in the middle of a period when he was composing the Suite, Op. 29, we would expect them to share many stylistic features with that work, and so they do. But, in addition, Schoenberg used these compositions as a testing-ground for new ideas. In particular, he looked for solutions to the problems of twelve-tone harmony. In these modest compositions, Schoenberg makes significant progress in his attempts to achieve harmonic integrity.

The first of these compositions, *Unentrinnbar* (Op. 27 No. 1), was completed on 30 September 1925. It is a brief (thirty-one-measure) four-voice composition for a cappella choir. The basic idea is quite simple: this is a four-voice canon with a short coda. The compositional materials are carefully limited: Schoenberg uses only two set forms, P-0 and I-5, with their retrogrades.

The canon begins with the soprano, followed at two-measure intervals by the remaining voices: first the alto with I-5, then the tenor, an octave below the soprano, and finally, the bass, an octave below the alto (see Ex. 6.1). Starting at m. 17 the voices begin to drop out and the bass voice brings the canon to a close in m. 23. This is followed by a brief coda, setting the last line of text.

Many of the stylistic features of this work are familiar, having been found in the compositions immediately preceding. The set is stated only

---

[1] The chronology follows Jan Maegaard, *Studien zur Entwicklung des dodekaphonen Satzes bei Arnold Schönberg*, 2 vols. and suppl. (Copenhagen, 1972), i. 121–3.

Ex. 6.1 Op. 27 No. 1, *Unentrinnbar*, mm. 1–12

as a line and, therefore, the four-voice structure is created by layering four different set forms in the four voices.

Moreover, the set, o e 8 2 1 7 9 t 4 3 5 6—like virtually all of its predecessors—is IH-combinatorial. But, as in the preceding works, Schoenberg does not combine IH-combinatorially related set forms to create aggregates. For example, the opening entries are arranged so that the initial hexachord of I-5 is placed, not opposite the initial hexachord of P-o, with which it would make an aggregate, but opposite the *second* hexachord of P-o. As a result, no aggregate is produced between this pair of voices. Instead, the soprano and the alto lines have the same pitch-class content in mm. 3–4.

To be sure, Schoenberg had important positive reasons for this combination. It is a feature of the ordering of this set that the last two elements of the second hexachord are the same as the first two elements of the IH-combinatorially related set form. Thus, the last notes of the second hexachord of P-o are B and C, the same as the first two notes of I-5. By arranging the entries so that the first two notes of I-5 occur together with the first four notes of the second hexachord of P-o, Schoenberg forms a collection equivalent to the second hexachord of P-o (or the first of I-5).[2]

None the less, even though Schoenberg did not exploit the properties of his set to produce 'harmonic' aggregates, it is clear that he was starting to make use of some of the other properties of IH-combinatoriality.

Prominent among those is the identity of pitch-class content of the disjunct hexachords of IH-combinatorially releated set forms. By using only P-o and I-5, Schoenberg ensured that there would be two and only two hexachords, in terms of pitch-class content. This is prerequisite to the development of the idea of hexachordal levels.

Moreover, each of the hexachords of a set relates in two ways to the hexachords of its IH-combinatorially related counterpart: as a permutation of the content of one, and an inversion of the intervals of the other.

Finally, the content of each individual line also suggests another way in which Schoenberg was beginning to recognize the compositional properties of IH-combinatoriality. In the canonic part of the work (mm. 1–23), each of the four voices states a set form and then its retrograde. Then the IH-combinatorially related form and its retrograde follow. As a result, at the joint between these two palindromes, a secondary set is created. Aggregates of this sort, formed between the hexachords of successive statements of IH-combinatorially related set forms, are an important feature of Schoenberg's mature style.

Thus, even though Schoenberg did not use the IH-combinatorial

[2] This is pointed out in Martha Hyde, 'A Theory of Twelve-Tone Meter', *Music Theory Spectrum*, 6 (1984), 17, 19.

properties of his set to create harmonic aggregates—as he would do in the mature compositions–he was beginning actively to exploit a range of associated properties.

One of the major issues facing Schoenberg in this period was the problem of harmony. Because Schoenberg tended to generate polyphony by layering multiple set forms, he ran into serious problems of harmonic consistency and cogency. Instead of presenting a clear harmonic profile, many passages from the pieces before this period seem opaque, with a tendency to create harmony more by negation—avoiding octaves, triads, and other tonal references—rather than by the constructive use of positive compositional principles.

In *Unentrinnbar*, as well as in the other choral pieces from this period, Schoenberg takes some clear steps to rectify this problem. Although this composition, like the Wind Quintet, Op.26, and the Suite, Op.29, generates polyphony by layering set forms, Schoenberg experiments with some techniques to control the intervallic relationships between the voices.

The canonic treatment of the voices is the most obvious of those techniques. By fixing the intervals, durations, and articulations, Schoenberg ensures that consistent harmonic relationships are created at metrically equivalent positions, every two measures. For example, compare the bottom three voices of m. 7 with the upper three voices in m. 5. All of the harmonic relationships are identical at corresponding moments in the respective measures. In each case, the opening trichord is pitch-class set 026; on the second eighth this becomes pitch-class set 027; on the second quarter it becomes pitch-class set 037, and so forth.

Beyond these consistent harmonic relationships, the canonical treatment of the voices has other important consequences. The canon in inversion ensures that identical durations, articulations, metric positions, and vowels are assigned to pairs of notes that are IN-5 related (Gb = o). For example, the first note in the soprano, is a Gb, occurs on the downbeat, lasts a dotted quarter, and has the syllable 'Tap-'. In m. 3 in the alto, the same duration, metric position, and syllable is assigned to the pitch B, the IN-5 counterpart of Gb. Since the index number is odd, it follows that there are six such pairs of pitch classes—Gb/B, F/C, E/C♯, Eb/D, Bb/G, A/G♯. Therefore, throughout the canon, where one note of these pairs occurs in one voice, the other note appears, with identical duration, articulation, and vowel in the inversionally related voice, two measures later.

In the coda, these pairings are made explicitly apparent in counterpoint, as the soprano and bass are paired together in contradistinction to a similar pairing in the alto and tenor. In mm. 24–9 the slightly skewed note-against-note counterpoint of these two pairings presents the IN-5 dyads established in the canon (see Ex. 6.2).

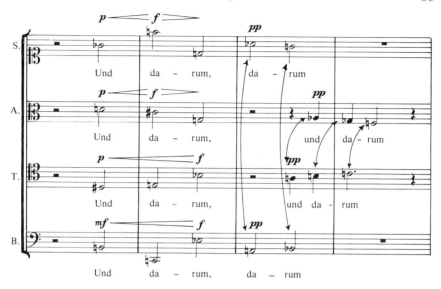

Ex. 6.2 Op. 27 No. 1, mm. 24–31: IN-5 dyads in the coda

Two weeks after completing Op. 27 No. 1, Schoenberg began work on what would be the third composition of the set, *Mond und Menschen*, finishing this brief composition two days later (16 October 1925). In many ways this work is virtually a clone of its predecessor. It uses a pair of IH-combinatorially related set forms and their retrogrades; secondary sets are created in the lines; the polyphony is generated by layering set forms; rotation is used. However, this work, unlike its predecessor, is not a canon. Instead, Schoenberg experiments with some other techniques in his effort to gain active control of the harmonic dimension.

The four lines of text are set to four disjunct musical phrases (mm. 1–6, 7–13, 14–20, 21–32), clearly set off from one another by fermatas. The first and second of these phrases are inversionally related. By means of this inversional relationship Schoenberg articulates some interesting harmonic procedures.

In the second phrase, every set form from the first phrase is replaced with its IH-combinatorially related counterpart (I-5 for P-0, P-0 for I-5). Moreover, the durations—except for some insignificant rearticulations—are precisely preserved. Finally, the spatial assignments are reversed, as well. For example, the bass voice of mm. 1–6 (assigned I-5) becomes the soprano voice in mm. 7–13 (assigned P-0), and vice versa. The same switching of roles takes place in the alto and tenor (see Ex. 6.3).

Since durations are preserved, both within each part, as well as in the relationship of the parts to one another, it follows that any harmony at any given point in the first phrase is duplicated at the equivalent spot in the second phrase. Thus, for example, in each case the opening dyad is interval class 3, the first trichord pitch-class set 014, and the first vertical tetrachord, pitch-class set 0147.

However, beyond these interval class relationships, Schoenberg's scheme also permits the preservation of the specific intervals themselves. Because the spatial relationships are inverted as well as the sets, it follows that all intervals, found at corresponding spots in the two phrases, are equivalent—not just in class, but in the specific interval as well. For example, the opening dyad, formed between the soprano and bass is a minor tenth. In the corresponding spot in the second phrase (m. 7), the same interval is produced: G♯ is in the bass and B in the soprano, again a minor tenth. The same holds for any pair of voices in any of the corresponding places in the two phrases.

The next composition, *Du sollst nicht*, Op.27 No. 2, was begun on 6 October 1925, and completed the next day. It has many of the characteristics of its two predecessors: it uses only two IH-combinatorially related sets; the polyphony is generated by layering linear set forms; rotation is a common technique; harmonic relationships are controlled by canonic procedures. Since these features have been discussed already, they need no further comment here. However, it is worth noting that, unlike the previous two works, Schoenberg does conjoin the order corresponding hexachords of IH-combinatorially related set forms. But, the aggregates created between such pairs of voices are localized within their constituent lines, to the exclusion of the two other

Ex. 6.3 Op. 27 No. 3, mm. 1–13: inversionally related phrases

Ex. 6.4 Op. 27 No. 2, mm. 5–8: aggregates formed in pairs of voices

parts (see Ex. 6.4). None the less, even though the aggregate-forming potential of IH-combinatoriality has not yet been systematically exploited, it should be clear that with every passing composition, it is becoming more and more inevitable.

The final piece of the opus, *Der Wunsch des Liebhabers*, occupied Schoenberg's attention for the next month and was completed on 10 November 1925. This interesting and engaging composition is a work of central importance in Schoenberg's development, representing one of those quantum leaps in thinking that characterize Schoenberg's self-inspired evolution. Though the largest composition of the set, it is not a long work, lasting a little more than three minutes. It does not have the formal complications of the Wind Quintet or the Suite, Op. 29. It is a modest composition, with carefully limited compositional aims. Yet, like all of the other compositions from this interlude, it faces the problem of twelve-tone harmony, and presents some persuasive solutions.

The set of this work is 0 2 9 5 7 3 t e 1 8 4 6. Throughout, Schoenberg partitions the set into three segments: order positions 0-4, 5-6, 7-e. The first and last segments provide the oriental flavour, for both are pentatonic scale collections. Moreover, the ordering of the set is such that the final pentachord is a transposition of the first down a half-step, a relationship made explicit from the first measure (see Ex. 6.5).

Although the hexachord of this set is IH-combinatorial, the set is never divided into hexachords, nor does Schoenberg use the IH-combinatorially related set form (I-1). Instead, Schoenberg uses I-5 as the counterpart of P-0. This choice is designed to exploit certain properties of the set, given the unvarying 5, 2, 5 partitioning.

The interval order within the pentachords is 2, 7, 8, 2. Thus, under the operation of retrograde inversion this becomes 2, 8, 7, 2, a kind of variation. That variational character is confirmed by the choice of I-5.

When the last pentachord of P-0 (C D A F G) is followed by the first pentachord of RI-5 (C D B♭ F G), as it is in the first two measures (see

Ex. 6.5 Op. 27 No. 4, mm. 1–2

Ex. 6.5, above), a two-tiered set of relationships is created. The first pentachord of RI-5 should be understood on two levels. On one hand, it is a retrograde inversion of the last pentachord of P-0. Therefore, we hear, in retrograde, the intervals of the prime form. On the other hand, this pentachord should also be understood as a variation of the last pentachord of P-0. The nearly invariant pitch-class content of the two pentachords is made explicit by preserving the registral, rhythmic, and order-position assignments of the invariant pitch classes.

In all the compositions of this opus Schoenberg attempted to deal with the harmonic problems posed by his twelve-tone method. Although each of the first three compositions had a unique way of approaching this problem, some significant common features may be observed: set choice was carefully limited to set forms closely related by the pitch-class content of their hexachords; the harmonic equivalence of the disjunct hexachords was continually stressed; the methods of set combination were controlled so that certain hexachords were consistently combined with others; rhythmic devices were employed to fix intervallic and chordal relationships between the voices. *Der Wunsch des Liebhabers*, although its set is not hexachordally divided, employs most of these techniques. However, in addition, it introduces some new and very significant ideas.[3]

The perpetual 5,2,5 partitioning of the set is, of course, a principal component of the harmonic consistency of this composition. Since the set is constructed so that both the first and last pentachords are pentatonic collections, it follows that the systematic use of this partitioning automatically creates a consistent succession of identical harmonies: pitch-class set 02479.

Moreover, this consistent partitioning into two equivalent penta-

---

[3] Schoenberg also noticed that this same pentachord is embedded in the set at order positions 0 3 4 5 6. In one sketch he beamed these together. See Hyde, 'The Format and Function of Schoenberg's Twelve-Tone Sketches', *Journal of the American Musicological Society*, 36 (1983), 457.

chords has other significant consequences. The pentatonic scale collection (pitch-class set 02479) is a collection generated by the four-fold application of interval class 5 from a given origin. As a result, its interval vector is {0, 3, 2, 1, 4, 0}. Therefore, interval class 5 is the most prominent interval within the collection, and the collection omits both the semitone and tritone.

Schoenberg exploits these properties to create a harmonic infrastructure that is very similar to the mature combinatorial harmony described in chapter 2: he divides the set into harmonically equivalent segments, characterized by a given intervallic content: then, by the consistent juxtaposition of these segments, he ensures that there will be a perceptible differentiation of harmonic function: the intervallic profile within the pentachords can be clearly distinguished from the intervallic profile formed between the pentachords (the difference vector).

The structure of the instrumental accompaniment is also important for the evolution of Schoenberg's ideas about twelve-tone harmonic structure. The accompanying instruments do not play set forms distinct from the chorus, nor do they slavishly double the choral parts. Instead, each of the four parts in the accompaniment takes the pitches of one of the segments of the 5, 2, 5 partitioning and presents those pitches in a freely repetitive manner. Thus, the instrumental parts are not bound to the ordering of the set, but instead present the pitch classes of the segments as *harmonic units*.

This marks an important turning-point in Schoenberg's twelve-tone thinking, for it encourages a more harmonic view of the set and of its constituent segments. The free reordering of the pitch classes of the pentachords allows the pentachords to be heard not just as an ordered series of pitch classes but, also, as harmonic units.

This harmonic treatment of the pentachords has metric consequences as well. As far back as the Suite, Op. 25, Schoenberg had learned how to use both the set as a whole and its constituent tetrachords to create a pitch-derived basis for metre. In Opp. 26 and 29, for the most part, this method of metric formation was suppressed because of the dense layering of set forms. In an environment where sets were piled, one on top of the other, without clear demarcation of their beginnings and endings, with the constant use of rotation, and the lack of congruence between the beginnings and endings of simultaneously stated set forms, it became impossible to express the metre by the simple, if effective, means used in the dance movements of Op. 25.

However, as soon as Schoenberg had developed new ways of generating polyphony, he immediately returned to a set-derived method of creating metre. The clear harmonic rhythm, made explicit by the accompaniment, articulates the metric units. The never-changing written metre indicates the referential metric norm that, in typical

Schoenberg style, is first established and then countered, returning at strategic locations.

In November 1925, having finished Op.27, Schoenberg began work on Op.28, the Three Satires, completing the three compositions by the end of the year. (There is also a non-serial appendix.) The first work of this opus, *Am Scheideweg*, is very similar to Op.27 No. 1. It is a four-voice canon with a coda, fixing the harmonic relationships through the rhythmic consistency. The beginning of the text ('Tonal oder atonal?') is, naturally, represented by assigning an arpeggiated triad to the word 'tonal' (C-E-G) and an atonal melody to the words 'oder atonal'. Op.28 No. 2, *Vielseitigkeit*, is not even a twelve-tone composition but, rather, an atonal take-off on Bach's Musical Offering, with a regrettable side-swipe at Stravinsky ('der kleine Modernsky'). Neither of these trifles represents serious advances in Schoenberg's stylistic development.

It is in the large composition of this set, *Der neue Klassizismus*, that Schoenberg makes his most serious efforts. This 'kleine Kantate' is the most ambitious and complicated, and the longest of any of the works of Opp.27–8, and represents a systematic attempt to apply the lessons learned in the previous compositions. Whereas the other choral pieces were relatively short in duration, limited in choice of set forms, circumscribed in their harmonic relationships, and modest in their compositional goals, *Der neue Klassizismus* is a full-blown composition, 181 measures in length (more than twice as long as any of the other compositions), ambitious in its formal, harmonic, and rhythmic domains. This composition represents the culmination of Schoenberg's efforts to gain positive control of the harmony.

The set of the composition, o e 1 9 3 7 t 8 2 6 4 5, is IH-combinatorial.

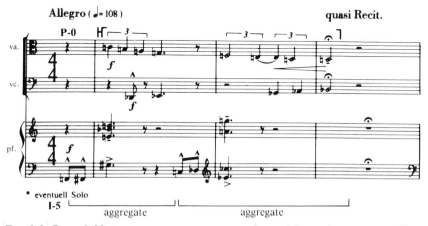

Ex. 6.6 Op. 28 No. 3, mm. 1–3: aggregates formed by order corresponding hexachords of IH-combinatorially related set forms

However, this composition, unlike its predecessors, makes full use of that property. Through the compositional techniques learned in the other compositions of Opp.27–28, Schoenberg prepared the way for the thoroughgoing use of IH-combinatoriality. The most significant single contribution of *Der neue Klassizismus* is its exploitation, in a systematic fashion, of the properties of combinatoriality—the use of IH-combinatorially related forms as the norm of local succession and association, their contrapuntal juxtaposition to form aggregates, their role in organizing the harmony, the exploitation of hexachordal levels to articulate the form, and the creation of a coherent, pitch-based metric. The systematic exploitation of these properties is one of the principal differences between Schoenberg's early and mature twelve-tone approaches. It is in this composition that Schoenberg begins to realize the enormous compositional potential of IH-combinatoriality.

The formation of aggregates by the juxtaposition of order corresponding hexachords of IH-combinatorially related set forms is apparent from the first measures of the composition (see Ex. 6.6).

With P-0 stated in the strings and I-5 in the piano, rests delineating the hexachords and parallel durational configurations emphasizing the hexachordal divisions, Schoenberg creates clearly defined aggregates. Although in some of the earlier compositions, aggregates had been formed between pairs of voices, those aggregates were often overlaid, and thus contradicted, by additional pitches in other voices. By contrast, aggregate formation in *Der neue Klassizismus* is coherent, consistent, and virtually thoroughgoing. It is not an occasional device, but the principal criterion for combining set forms.

The systematic exploitation of IH-combinatoriality has a significance that goes far beyond the formation of aggregates. It is a mark of the thoroughness of Schoenberg's compositional thinking that, simultaneous with his systematic use of this property to create aggregates, he also found ways to apply this technique in other domains as well.

As described in Chapter 2, Schoenberg's mature harmony was characterized by the systematic use of what was termed combinatorial harmony. Given the normative division of the set into hexachords, the harmonic equivalence of the disjunct hexachords in IH-combinatorial sets, and the pitch-class complementation of the order corresponding hexachords, it was possible to create a referential and pervasive set of intervallic relationships, determined by the particular structure of the set: intervals most prominent within the hexachord are rarest between the hexachords and vice versa.

In the present instance (see Ex. 6.6, above) this is clearly audible. The hexachord, pitch-class set 023468, has the interval vector {2, 4, 2, 4, 1, 2 }. Therefore, the thirty-six intervals formed between the two hexachords are described by the difference vector {8, 4, 8, 4, 10, 2}.

Taking only interval classes 1 and 5, which are rare within the hexa-chords, one can see that those very intervals appear pervasively between the hexachords, relationships that are emphasized and clari-fied by the instrumentation.

Moreover, the formation of aggregates between IH-combinatorially related set forms permitted Schoenberg to continue his efforts to forge persuasive connections between the pitch structure and the metre. This is evident from the beginning of the composition, where the metre—equivalent to the written metre—originates from the regular succession of aggregates. With this discovery, we have arrived at the mature treat-ment of metre in Schoenberg's twelve-tone music: the metre is formed by the periodicity of the aggregate along the time line. (Of course, as in all of Schoenberg's music, the establishment of an initial metre is not treated as invariable, but rather as a norm that provides material for further development).

Finally, in addition to its impact on the harmonic and metric organ-ization, Schoenberg's use of IH-combinatoriality had an immediate effect on the formal structure.

It should be recalled that as soon as Schoenberg gained the requisite compositional skills with his new method he launched into two remark-ably ambitious and exceptionally complicated large-scale composi-tions: the Quintet, Op. 26, and the Suite, Op. 29. In those works he developed some interesting solutions to the problem of twelve-tone form. We have seen that throughout his serial period, Schoenberg, having faced a problem in one piece, and then, in later compositions, having developed new skills and techniques, returns to that problem and refines his previous solution. Such is the case with the formal organization of this composition. Having developed the idea of IH-combinatoriality, he returns to apply it to the problem of twelve-tone form.

With a few exceptions, Schoenberg restricts set-form combinations to IH-combinatorially related forms. An immediate consequence is that for each pair of such set forms there are two, and only two, hexachords in terms of their pitch-class content. This permits the establishment of hexachordal levels. These play a central role in the form, for the hexa-chordal levels articulate the formal divisions.

In this composition P-0 and I-5 are the only set forms used in the first fifty-one measures of the composition—nearly a third of the work: Schoenberg has established a referential hexachordal level for the com-position, a referential norm that he treats as somewhat analogous to the tonic region in a tonal composition. After moving away to other regions in mm. 52–74, Schoenberg returns to this referential region in prepara-tion for the next major section of the composition, the fugue that begins in m. 87. Once again, P-0 and I-5 are the only set forms used until m.

101. Then, after another detour to transitory secondary regions, P-0 and I-5 return as the set forms of the final section of the composition, mm. 153–81.

Moreover, it is the structure of the set that helps determine the intervals of transposition used for the secondary regions. The interval vector shows the relative rarity of interval class 5 within the hexachord. Thus, if we compare P-0 to P-7 (or to P-5) we see that by the common tone theorem, the hexachords of sets so related will have but one pitch class in common in corresponding hexachords. It follows that the IH-combinatorially related counterpart of P-7—I-0, of course, will have five pitch classes in common with the corresponding hexachords of P-0. This acts as a determinant for the choice of secondary areas, for it is this property that is exploited in the form of this composition.

The concept of the referential set form has been an idea that Schoenberg exploited as early as *Die Jakobsleiter* in 1917. However, we can see that Schoenberg has returned to this familiar idea, improved it, deepened its significance, and strengthened its systematic consistency. To establish as referential a group of set forms that do not share common hexachordal pitch-class content is hardly a methodological error in a composition where the idea of hexachordal combinatoriality is not exploited. But, as soon as Schoenberg learned to draw upon that particular resource for the creation of local aggregates, the control of local harmony, and the fostering of a pitch-derived metric, he immediately recognized its formal potential. He returned to the problem of twelve-tone form and, armed with his new technique of IH-combinatoriality, refined the solutions of Opp. 26 and 29. With its mature exploitation of hexachordal levels to articulate and differentiate the formal sections, *Der neue Klassizismus* offers eloquent testimony to the thoroughness of Schoenberg's musical thinking.

With the completion of Op. 28, Schoenberg closed out an important stage in his development. In these modest little pieces Schoenberg set for himself a single task: to gain positive control of the harmonic organization of his twelve-tone method. Using a variety of different approaches, Schoenberg learned to do exactly that. But, as so often in his odyssey, the solution to one problem had profound consequences: in these choral works Schoenberg not only faced the problem of twelve-tone harmony, but at the same time, learned how to apply those harmonic ideas to create aggregates, structure the metre, and articulate the form.

7

The Art of Twelve-tone Composition
The String Quartet No. 3 and the Variations for Orchestra,
1926–1928

In the spring of 1926, when Schoenberg began working on the Variations for Orchestra, he had been a serial composer for six years. During that learning period he had completed a number of twelve-tone works and, in the process, discovered a wide range of useful techniques.

However, it is with the compositions from this period, the String Quartet No. 3, Op.30, and especially the Variations for Orchestra, Op.31, that Schoenberg finally began to realize in the most successful way the possibilities of his new method. These compositions are the culmination of his learning period; here Schoenberg introduced the last of his mature techniques and, even more significantly, discovered how they could be integrated into a comprehensive musical system.

Once again the chronology is anything but simple. Schoenberg sketched ideas for the Variations for Orchestra as early as March 1926.[1] He began working in earnest several months later, completing about half the composition before breaking off. Then, sometime near the beginning of 1927, he turned instead to a new composition, the String Quartet No. 3, Op.30. He worked at a fast pace on this new work, completing it two months later (8 March 1927). Schoenberg returned to the Variations in 1928, completing them in September of that year.[2]

Up to this point, when there were chronological complications, we have discussed first those compositions that were started first. To be consistent we should turn now to the Variations for Orchestra. However, since certain techniques of the String Quartet No. 3 represent a cul-de-sac, while the Variations—and in particular that part written after Schoenberg resumed work in 1928—more fully anticipate the future course of his twelve-tone development, we will begin with the String Quartet No. 3.

[1] Originally he entitled the work Passacaglia for Orchestra. Owing to a badly written '6' in the date '1926' it had been assumed that the Passacaglia stemmed from the year 1920. However, this fragment is surely from 1926. See my 'Redating Schoenberg's Passacaglia for Orchestra', *Journal of the American Musicological Society*, 40 (1987), 471–94.

[2] The chronology follows Jan Maegaard, *Studien zur Entwicklung des dodekaphonen Satzes bei Arnold Schönberg*, 2 vols. and suppl. (Copenhagen, 1972), i. 124–5, with the emendation that the beginning date of the Orchestra Variations was Mar. 1926, the date of the Passacaglia.

By the time of the compositions immediately preceding this period Schoenberg had developed many of the mature twelve-tone techniques. However, as late as the Suite, Op.29, and some of the choral pieces, Opp.27–8, Schoenberg persisted in relying on strictly linear presentations of the set, a technique that can be traced back to the earliest serial experiments.

Several of the most characteristic features of the early period—rotation, subsidiary sets, and layering—were direct consequences of this pervasive reliance on linear set presentations. Moreover, one of the biggest problems of those compositions—the obscurity of harmonic relationships—results from the piling up of set forms without a systematic basis for that combination.

The renunciation of a primarily linear view of the set occurs during this period. In its place Schoenberg begins to make partitioned sets the norm of local set presentation, and reserves strictly linear presentations of the set for significant points in the formal structure. As so often before, this important change in his compositional technique does not take place in isolation. Rather, in the process of learning to deal with this new method of set presentation, Schoenberg transforms his thinking about a myriad of other features as well.

The String Quartet No. 3, like several of its predecessors, uses more than one set. However, unlike Opp.26 and 29 where the subsidiary sets were generated by partitioning out elements from a succession of local statements of the principal set, here Schoenberg begins the composition with clear statements of the different sets. (Schoenberg's next composition, *Von Heute auf Morgen*, Op.32, also uses more than one set.) In the present instance, Schoenberg used three sets—or, more precisely, one principal set with two ordering variants (see Ex. 7.1).

principal set: 0 9 8 2 5 t e 4 3 6 1 7

variant A: 0 9 8 2 5 6 1 t 4 e 7 3

variant B: 0 9 8 2 5 6 3 1 t e 4 7

Ex. 7.1 String Quartet No. 3: the three sets

The motivation for the use of multiple orderings of the set was probably related to Schoenberg's continuing concern that he might not be able to build up an entire composition from a single set. However, at the same time that he was relying on multiple sets to provide sufficient variety, he was also methodically learning the very techniques that would make the use of such multiple orderings unnecessary. In the String Quartet No. 3 and the Variations for Orchestra Schoenberg learned the compositional techniques that would permit him 'to draw themes' from the set with sufficient flexibility that he would have no need of multiple orderings.[3]

Schoenberg approached this problem by setting careful limitations on the methods of presenting the set. In marked contrast to the compositions before 1926, he virtually eschews linear presentations of the set in the String Quartet No. 3. With the exception of the third movement, straightforward linear presentations are strictly limited to strategic locations. In the first movement, for example, there are no purely linear presentations of the set for the first sixty-one measures. Moreover, unlike the earlier compositions, there is no layering of set forms in this composition; that has now been abandoned as a compositional technique. Indeed, for the most part—excepting only the second movement—Schoenberg virtually avoids the polyphonic combination of set forms. With occasional exceptions, the norm of set presentation in this composition is a single partitioned set—a radical transformation of his compositional technique.

The abandonment of linear set statements as the norm of set presentation posed serious compositional challenges for Schoenberg. When the set is stated as a line there is a one-to-one relationship between the melody and the structure of the set. Yet, when the set is broken up and partitioned into several voices the resultant linear events may or may not be equivalent to segments of the set. This prompts a difficult compositional question: what relationship can or should these extracted segments bear to the presumably referential set? Schoenberg in facing—and solving—this problem made another one of those quantum leaps in thinking that were to transform, irrevocably, his application of twelve-tone technique.

For example, in the passage beginning in m. 76, Schoenberg has presented a succession of local set forms, grouped into pairs by the alternation of prime and inversional forms, and by the fixed durational patterns (see Ex. 7.2).

In the local set forms, the material within each line is a discrete segment of the set. For instance, in the first set form of the passage, P-7 in mm. 76-7, the first violin states order positions 0-1, the cello 2-4, the viola 5-8 (in retrograde), and the second violin 9-e (also in retrograde).

However, these segments are not heard in isolation. The grouping of set forms into pairs ensures that the short melodic fragments within the voices will coalesce into longer units, composed of elements of two successive, I-related set forms.

---

[3] Referring to the set of *Moses und Aron*, Schoenberg remarked that 'the more familiar I became with this set the more easily I could draw themes from it.' See 'Composition with Twelve Tones (1)', in *Style and Idea*, ed. Leonard Stein, trans. Leo Black (New York, 1975), 224.

Ex 7.2 String Quartet No. 3, first movement, mm. 76–95

Thus, in the first violin, D and B from P-7, in mm. 76–7, are grouped together with the following dyad, F♯-E♯, into a unit.

The specific grouping of elements from successive local set forms reveals the great distance travelled in Schoenberg's serial odyssey. The tetrachords formed by this pairing of set forms are carefully structured to present elements from the governing set on a higher level. These tetrachords do not result from the arbitrary conjunction of elements of disparate set forms, but are instead middleground structures that result from careful planning and selection. Every aspect of the compositional design is crucial here—the choice of partitioning, the assignment of segments into specific voices, the rhythms employed, the set forms chosen.

For instance, the tetrachord in the first violin in mm. 76–9, D B F♯ E♯, pitch-class set 0147 is embedded in the set twice: at order positions 1–4 and 3–6. Thus, the melodic structure formed by the conjunction of elements of successive set statements is equivalent to embedded harmonies of the set.

This example has not been selectively chosen to prove a point; to the contrary, *every tetrachord* in the first violin—the *Hauptstimme*—in mm. 76–94 is harmonically equivalent to an embedded segment of the principal set or of its two variants.[4] These structures are not coincidental, but conscious efforts to present the set in several dimensions.

The impact of this discovery is both immediate and profound. With this new technique Schoenberg was no longer constrained by a limited view of how the set could be presented. The set could be partitioned into various voices, thus generating the polyphony, yet at the same time the melodic structures created within those individual lines could be derived from the structure of the set.

Moreover, since the use of partitioned sets freed him from the limitations of strictly linear set presentations, Schoenberg no longer felt it necessary to use the primitive techniques of rotation for melodic variety or layering to generate polyphony. These techniques now disappear from Schoenberg's vocabulary, never to return: they had served their purpose in the earliest compositions, but now could be replaced by methods that were much more effective. The systematic exploitation of the possibilities of partitioned sets thus had an impact far beyond the level of detail.

The creation of middleground structures was not limited to segments harmonically equivalent to embedded segments of the set. Rather, Schoenberg demonstrated his interest in a wide range of such structures.

---

[4] A♭ B♭ D♭ C, mm. 77–81 and G F♯ A B mm. 88–90 = pitch-class set 0135, embedded in Variant B, order positions 6–9; A D♯ E G, mm. 82–4 and C E♭ E B♭, mm. 85–7 = pitch-class set 0146, embedded in all three sets, order positions 0–3; D C♯ G♯ F, mm. 91–3 = pitch-class set 0147, embedded in order positions 1–4 of all three sets and order positions 3–6 of the principal set.

Ex. 7.3 String Quartet No. 3, first movement, mm. 62–75

For example, in mm. 62–75, the passage immediately preceding the previous example, Schoenberg presents, for the first time in the composition, the set as a line in a voice (see Ex. 7.3). In mm. 62–8, the first violin, the *Hauptstimme*, presents I-5, subdivided by a rest into hexachords. Immediately following, in mm. 69–75, the other principal set form of the composition P-0, appears in retrograde in the same voice. These two linear presentations have been carefully reserved for an important point in the formal structure: this is the second principal theme of the movement.

In Ex. 7.3 the principal voice states the set in a straightforward linear presentation. However, these set statements are themselves generated as a result of the conjunction of elements from a succession of local set forms. Those local forms are not randomly chosen, but rather, are determined by the structure of the set and the partitionings used.[5]

The principal set of this Quartet is 0 9 8 2 5 t e 4 3 6 1 7. This set has the property that within the six discrete dyads there are only three different interval classes, one of each class in each of the two hexachords: interval class 3 (dyads 1 and 5), interval class 6 (dyads 2 and 6), and interval class 5 (dyads 3 and 4) (see Ex. 7.4).

the set: 0   9 8   2 5   t e   4 3   6 1   7

interval class of the dyads: 3   6   5   5   3   6

Ex. 7.4 Interval classes in the dyades of the principal set of Op. 30

From the beginning of the first movement Schoenberg establishes as normative the subdivision of the set into three segments, composed of 5, 5, and 2 elements respectively. The 5, 5, 2 (or 5, 2, 5) subdivision in conjunction with the two variants of the principal set determine local set choice for the multidimensional set presentation.

In order to generate the first two notes of the melody, C–E♭—interval class 3—Schoenberg needed to use a 5, 2, 5 segmentation of Variant B of the set (see Ex. 7.5). Of the transformations of Variant B, two

Variant B; 0 9 8 2 5   6 3   1 t e 4 7

interval class 3————

Ex. 7.5 Variant B of Op. 30, segmented 5, 2, 5 to produce interval class 3

place C and E♭ in the central dyad (order positions 5–6): P-2 and I-e (see Ex. 7.6). Of these two options Schoenberg chooses I-e (Variant B).

---

[5] A brief discussion of this aspect of this passage is in Martha Hyde, 'A Theory of Twelve-Tone Meter', *Music Theory Spectrum*, 6 (1984), 38.

P-2: A F♯ F B D   E♭ C   B♭ G G♯ C♯E
I-e F♯ AB♭ E C♯   C E♭   F G♯ G D B

Ex. 7.6 Set forms that place C-E♭ in the central dyad under the 5, 2, 5 segmentation of Variant B:

The next two notes of the evolving principal line are E-B♭, a dyad of interval class 6. In order to produce this dyad, he must use a 5, 5, 2 segmentation of the principal set. Since the set form used to generate the previous dyad was an inversion, here Schoenberg must use a prime form if he is to preserve the privileged hierarchical standing of the evolving principal line. P-2 and P-8 place E and B♭ in the appropriate order positions, and Schoenberg chooses P-2.

The next dyad, G-D—interval class 5—demands a 5, 2, 5 segmentation of Variant A. In keeping with the patterns set in the previous two set statements, this must be an inversion: Schoenberg uses I-1.

With the G-D dyad we have completed the first hexachord of the set. The second hexachord of the slowly unfolding line is generated in precisely the same way: each dyad is extracted from the appropriate variant using the 5, 5, 2 or 5, 2, 5 segmentation.

The set appears here in several dimensions. At the local level, there is a succession of partitioned statements of the set. At the same time, the principal voice is formed by the extraction of a dyad from each of those local set forms.

A closely related procedure—the construction of middleground aggregates—is also a prominent feature of the String Quartet No. 3. To be sure, the foundation for this idea was laid in Schoenberg's prior compositions. In both the Wind Quintet, Op.26, and the Suite, Op.29, Schoenberg extracted elements from a succession of local set statements to produce a subsidiary set.

In the String Quartet No. 3, Schoenberg returns to that idea. But now, no longer constrained by the need to produce a subsidiary set, he introduces the more general concept of the middleground, linear aggregate.

For example, an aggregate is formed in mm. 19–22 of the third movement (see Ex. 7.7). In each of the four measures of the example, Schoenberg presents a partitioned set statement. At the same time, in the principal voice, the first violin, an aggregate unfolds, three notes from each of the four local set statements.

This middleground, linear aggregate binds the passage together as a unit. Each of the local set statements makes perfect sense at the level of detail. Yet, at the same time, a higher-level structure is formed from elements of these local set statements. From this point on such middleground aggregates are to be a central feature of Schoenberg's twelve-tone style.

Ex. 7.7 A linear aggregate generated by the conjunction of elements from a succession of local set forms

Middleground aggregates, multidimensional set presentations, and embedded set segments are all dependent on the use of partitioned sets. And, from this point on in Schoenberg's development, the partitioned set becomes the norm of set presentation. Moreover, the pervasive use of partitioned set statements brings about a fundamental change in Schoenberg's conceptualization of the twelve-tone system. In an environment where the set is constantly presented in partitioning, the referential ordering cannot be inferred from every presentation of the set. Rather, the set becomes the referential background of the composition, not a constantly reiterated foreground. With this change, Schoenberg has completed the transformation of the serial idea, from its origins as a kind of motive to something far more abstract and thus far more flexible in its application.

The pervasive use of partitioned sets had other significant consequences as well.

As early as the Variations from the Serenade, Op.24, Schoenberg discovered how to use isomorphic partitioning. This technique appears in virtually every subsequent composition, but since the norm of set presentation was the linear statement of the set, isomorphic partitioning was only an occasional device.

This changes completely in the period under consideration. Since the norm of set presentation in the Quartet is the partitioned set, and since strictly linear presentations are limited to carefully chosen strategic locations, isomorphic partitioning became a logical method of relating local set statements to one another.

That is precisely what Schoenberg does. He takes a technique developed in the earliest days of his serial period and turns it into a central feature of his compositional vocabulary. Isomorphic partitioning is no longer limited to a few isolated passages, but instead it becomes a pervasive feature, effecting a majority of the set presentations.

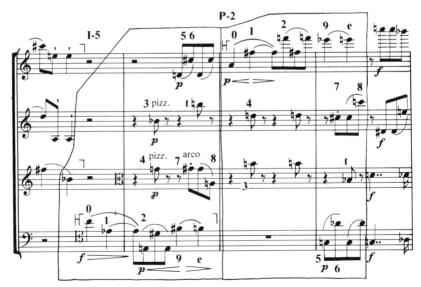

Ex. 7.8 String Quartet No. 3, fourth movement, mm. 53–6: I-5 and P-2, isomorphically partitioned

The thoroughgoing use of isomorphic partitioning had other consequences. In the earlier serial compositions Schoenberg tended to construct the set so that one of the transformations would slightly vary the ordering of a segment of the original. The sets of the Wind Quintet and the Suite, Op. 29, both had this feature. However, with the extensive use of partitioning, Schoenberg sought out methods of producing invariant relationships through the partitioning, and not through the strict linear ordering of the set. As a result, from this point on, Schoenberg changes the way he constructs his sets. No longer are the sources of developing variation to be found in the strict linear ordering of the set but, rather, in the transformations and relationships that can be brought out by isomorphic partitioning.

Moreover, Schoenberg exploited the virtual saturation of the surface with isomorphically partitioned sets to control phrase construction.

For example, in mm. 53–6, in the final movement, Schoenberg presents a partitioned statement of I-5 followed by an isomorphically partitioned statement of P-2 (see Ex. 7.8). Since these two set statements are isomorphically partitioned, and since Schoenberg fixes both the durations, as well as the metric position of all elements of equivalent order position in the two forms, he creates a compelling logical basis for the phrase structure.

Since each segment in the second set form is an inversion of a segment from the first, there is a clear system of pattern completion. As each partitioned segment from the second set unfolds, it relates to the inversionally identical patterns from the first set form. Thus, when each of the partitioned segments from the second set form is harmonically equivalent to the corresponding segment from the first form, the phrase is complete.

Here again, as in so many other domains, we see Schoenberg searching for ways to apply his new method to all dimensions of the musical surface. The phrases are formed, not by the *ad hoc* segmentation of the musical continuum, but by the methodical exploitation of the properties of the twelve-tone system.

In one sense the String Quartet No. 3 might seem to represent a detour in Schoenberg's path of stylistic development. In the compositions immediately preceding, the mature properties of IH-combinatoriality gradually emerged, culminating with *Der neue Klassizismus*, where IH-combinatorially related sets were used as the norm of local set association and combination, with the resultant systematic formation of aggregates and manipulation of hexachordal levels.

Neither the principal set of the String Quartet No. 3, nor the two variants are IH-combinatorial. However, that does not mean that Schoenberg was considering abandoning IH-combinatoriality as an essential feature of his twelve-tone technique. For one thing, in the first,

third, and final movements, Schoenberg virtually avoids the polyphonic combination of set statements. Moreover, in the second movement,
Schoenberg continued his examination of the problem of combinatoriality. However, in this movement Schoenberg experiments, not with
IH-combinatoriality but, rather, with R-combinatoriality.[6]

The second movement is a set of double variations, with mm. 1-10
providing the first idea, mm. 11–20 the second. In the occurrences of
the second idea Schoenberg experiments with R-combinatoriality (see
Ex. 7.9).

In each measure of the example Schoenberg has presented two retrograde related set forms. In m. 11, I-5 is partitioned between the first
violin and viola, while its retrograde, RI-5, appears in the second violin

Ex. 7.9 String Quartet No. 3, second movement, mm. 11–15

I-5: C Eb E Bb G D Db Ab A Gb B F   (partitioned between vc. and vn. 2, in m. 11)
RI-5: F B Gb A Ab C♯ D G A♯ E Eb C   (partitioned between vn. 1 and va. in m. 11)

---

[6] A detailed analysis of this movement is given in Steven Peles, 'Interpretations of Sets in Multiple Dimensions: Notes on the Second Movement of Arnold Schoenberg's *String Quartet #3*', *Perspectives of New Music*, 22 (1983–4), 303–52.

and cello. The two set forms are clearly differentiated by articulation and rhythm.

As a result of this combination, two harmonic aggregates are formed for each pair of R-related set forms. But these aggregates are not always formed strictly by hexachords. For instance, the first aggregate formed in m. 11 involves four pitch classes from RI-5 and eight from I-5.

If octaves are to be avoided between R-related sets then the rate of unfolding of the two sets must be carefully controlled. For example, during the time one set form has presented order positions 0-8, the R-related form can state only order positions e, t, and 9. If it goes past 9, octaves will result.

One consequence of these constraints is the consistent formation of a kind of voice exchange. For instance, in m. 11, A and A♭ are exchanged between the cello and viola, in m. 12, D and C♯ switch between the viola and second violin.

Perhaps the constraints posed by these constant near-octaves convinced Schoenberg that R-combinatoriality did not have the potential of IH-combinatoriality. In any event, R-combinatoriality was abandoned as a compositional procedure after this composition. None the less, its presence here offers compelling evidence of Schoenberg's fascination with the idea of combinatoriality and the aggregate.

In some ways the String Quartet No. 3 is an oddity in Schoenberg's development. The multiple sets and the use of R-combinatoriality are ideas that did not become a fixed part of his compositional arsenal. However, it would be a mistake to see this work as an aberration, as something standing essentially outside the mainstream of Schoenberg's evolving serial thinking. Rather, this work poses certain problems, and proposes certain solutions that contribute directly to the final refinements that Schoenberg was to make in his now almost completely mature handling of his serial system.[7]

Schoenberg began work on the Variations for Orchestra, Op.31, in the spring of 1926. At first he titled the composition 'Passacaglia for Orchestra'. By 5 March 1926 he had worked out a set and sketched the beginning of the Passacaglia. This fragment—like the String Quartet No. 3—uses more than one set: there are two orderings of the second hexachord. However, Schoenberg shortly abandoned this idea, and by May 1926 he had decided upon a new, single ordering. He had completed nearly half of the composition when he interrupted the Variations for

---

[7] For a completely different view of Schoenberg's application of the twelve-tone system see Christian Möllers, *Reihentechnik und musikalische Gestalt bei Arnold Schönberg: eine Untersuchung zum III. Streichquartett op. 30* Beihefte zum Archiv für Musikwissenschaft, xvii (Wiesbaden, 1977). Möllers concludes that the actual musical surface bears no relationship to the twelve-tone method and can be understood perfectly adequately without reference to it. He asserts that Schoenberg's twelve-tone technique may best be thought of as a composer's secret, without real significance for the apprehension and understanding of the musical work by others.

the String Quartet No. 3. He returned and completed the Variations by September 1928.

The Variations for Orchestra are Schoenberg's first complete orchestral composition since the Five Pieces, Op. 16, written nearly twenty years earlier. Here for the first time is his inimitable twelve-tone orchestral sound, a product of the renunciation of octave doubling and the careful limitation to unison doubling. Although the importance of this orchestrational practice has been exaggerated—Schoenberg abandoned this limitation in the Piano Concerto, Op. 42—it is a highly characteristic sound and it should be understood as an indication of the degree of his concern about the tonal implications of the octave during that period.[8]

Formally, Op. 31 is divided into an Introduction, Theme, nine variations, and a Finale (which is nearly as long as the rest of the composition). The 520 measures of this composition constitute the most extended individual movement of his twelve-tone period to date. By any standards it is one of Schoenberg's most ambitious compositions.

It has been mentioned that the Variations constitute 'a veritable "Art of the Fugue" of early twelve-tone technique.'[9] This remark, dropped almost casually in a discussion of another work, should be taken very seriously. Not only are there obvious general parallels but, also, there is the explicit B-A-C-H theme that becomes the focus of the Finale. Can it be coincidental then that Schoenberg's set, at its original pitch level, contains a five-note segment that seems as if it could be used to form a theme for another Contrapunctus? (see Ex. 7.10).

Ex. 7.10 Variations for Orchestra, Op. 31: the theme

Taken in isolation this resemblance might seem a bit far-fetched, but when it is seen together with the B-A-C-H motive, the appearance in the sketches of Bach-like fugal episodes in D minor,[10] and the prominent role Bach's Art of the Fugue played in Schoenberg's pedagogy in

---

[8] 'To double is to emphasize, and an emphasized tone could be interpreted as a root, or even as a tonic; the consequences of such an interpretation must be avoided. Even a slight reminiscence of the former tonal harmony would be disturbing, because it would create false expectations of consequences and continuations.' See 'Composition with Twelve Tones (1)', 219.

[9] Milton Babbitt, 'Three Essays on Schoenberg', in Benjamin Boretz and Edward Cone (edd.), *Perspectives on Schoenberg and Stravinsky* (rev. edn., New York, 1972), 53.

[10] See for example the sketch-pages numbered 1636 and 1639 in the archives of the Arnold Schoenberg Institute.

the early 1920s, it should be clear that the Variations represented Schoenberg's homage to that composer whose music had done so much to assure the importance of German music in a previous century.[11]

The Variations are no superficial recycling of classical variation form: Schoenberg was not turning back to an anachronistic or sentimental exploitation of the external features of a bygone era. Rather, the Variations represent Schoenberg's most compelling and consistent experiment in twelve-tone organization to date.

INTRODUCTION

The Introduction lasts thirty-three measures and succinctly presents many of the important melodic, harmonic, thematic, and rhythmic issues that will be developed over the course of the work.

Part of the purpose of the Introduction is to establish at the beginning of the composition not merely the referential set of the composition but, just as important, harmonic norms that result from specific, carefully limited combinations of set forms: the IH-combinatorial pairing.

Although the concept of a referential set form, or group of set forms, has been current since as far back as *Die Jakobsleiter*, not until the harmonic refinements introduced in Opp. 27 and 28 was there a systematic formula for set combinations. In the mature period it is impossible to consider the properties of Schoenberg's sets in isolation, but only in context of the juxtaposition of IH-combinatorially related pairs.

The consequences of this kind of thinking are apparent from the first measures of the introduction (see Ex. 7.11). The canonic imitation—a resonance of the rhythmic procedures of Opp. 27–8—produces a 0369 tetrachord. This is not a segment of the set, but rather a harmony that occurs through the combination of a set form with its IH-combinatorial counterpart.

This harmony, stated at the beginning of the introduction, will be a recurrent and central harmonic motto, returning at strategic points in the structure of the piece, influencing the choice of set forms for combination.

Within the set are two tritones: between order positions 0–1 and 7–8. The tetrachord formed by these two tritones is pitch-class set 0369 and for both P-0 and I-9 the specific pitch level of this tetrachord is the same

---

[11] Interleaved in Schoenberg's copy of the *Art of Fugue*, preserved in the archives of the Arnold Schoenberg Institute, are a number of pages that show the central position this work played in Schoenberg's pedagogy of the early 1920s. On one sheet someone wrote out his students' names and the specific Contrapunctus each was to prepare. These students—Deutsch, Eisler, Rankl, Kalteborn, Travnicek, Novikoff—studied with Schoenberg between 1918 and 1923. The years common to all of the students mentioned were 1919 to 1921, so these sheets must stem from that period.

Introduktion

Ex. 7.11 Variations for Orchestra, Op. 31: the beginning of the Introduction with the 0369 tetrachord

as the tetrachord formed between these two forms in the first four measures.

Schoenberg uses this property to determine the transpositions in mm. 17–23. Up to m. 17 Schoenberg had used only the IH-combinatorial pair of set forms, P-0 and I-9. Starting in m. 17 Schoenberg proceeds through a number of set forms: I-0, P-6, I-6, I-9, R-3, RI-3, P-9. These forms are chosen because all of them produce the same tetrachord in order positions 0–1, 7–8: C♯ E G B♭, the harmonic motto of mm. 1–4. This tetrachord, and its component tritones, pervade mm. 17–23.

Thus, Schoenberg has determined two levels of hierarchy in set choice. At one level are the IH-combinatorially related set forms, with P-0 and I-9 receiving referential priority. At a more general level is that group of forms, P-0, P-3, P-6, P-9, I-0, I-3, I-6, and I-9, that produce the C♯-E-G-B♭ tetrachord out of their embedded tritones.

Ex. 7.12 Variations for Orchestra, Op. 31, mm. 23–8: the B-A-C-H theme at mm. 24–5 in the Introduction

This opening is remarkable, as well, for its exposition of the material. Here the first hexachords of P-o and I-9 are introduced together, unfolding slowly in a quasi-canon over the first ten measures. The individual elements of the set appear gradually, each time circling back over previous elements of the hexachord. Thus, we might best think of the linear statement of the set as emerging from the hexachord, which must be thought of as the referential background. With the complete statement of the two IH-combinatorially related hexachords, Schoenberg has introduced not only the referential linear norms but at the same time has established the basic components of his harmonic and aggregate formation as well.

Immediately following, after a brief ritard, Schoenberg introduces another idea that is to be of central importance in the course of the work: the B-A-C-H theme (see Ex. 7.12). This theme is no foreign object, grafted on to a twelve-tone work, but a logical relation, originating in the structure of the set itself. Schoenberg has managed to quote from the past while preserving the consistency of his method.

The B-A-C-H theme is formed by the conjunction of elements from two consecutive set forms, P-o and I-1, stated in mm. 24 and 25 respectively. These two forms are isomorphically partitioned, with order positions o and 5 placed in the trombone, forming the theme.

The particular structure of Schoenberg's partitioning has a number of profound consequences. The extraction of order positions o and 5 from the first hexachord leaves four order positions: 1–4. For P-o Schoenberg places order positions 2 and 4 in the cello and order positions 1 and 3 in the cor anglais. For RI-1, he reverses those assignments.

The instrumental assignments reveal immediately the invariance of this tetrachord. Moreover, this tetrachord is pitch-class set 0123, the same as the B-A-C-H theme. Thus, Schoenberg's partitioning emphasizes the harmonic equivalence of the B-A-C-H theme to a segment of the set. The 0123 tetrachord is formed in the trombone as the result of the conjunction of elements from several set forms and, at the same time, in the accompaniment as a segment of the set statement. This is emphasized by the invariant content of the accompanying tetrachords.

Certainly the B-A-C-H theme is a reference to a prior era, but it has been made to fit within the confines not only of the twelve-tone system but within the logic of this particular composition. In Schoenberg's hands it has become not an arbitrary quote but an event, intimately related to and derived from the structure of the set.

THEME

Although the Introduction has set in motion a number of the important harmonic and motivic ideas of the composition, the set itself has not yet been stated as a melodically complete unit. That is the central role of the next section, the Theme.

Starting in m. 34 Schoenberg states the IH-combinatorial four-group of set forms in a straightforward linear presentation: P-0, RI-9, R-0, I-9. Here, in explicit form, are the fundamental referential building-blocks of the composition. Moreover, as is normative for Schoenberg's compositions from this point onward, each of these set forms is accompanied by its IH-combinatorial counterpart. Thus, Schoenberg establishes a referential group of set forms for the composition, as well as the norm of set combination: IH-combinatoriality.

In the individual set statements, Schoenberg subdivides the set into shorter segments, usually 5, 4, and 3 elements. This segmentation is an important part of the rhythmic organization of the theme, and will reappear in several of the variations.

VARIATION I

Although IH-combinatoriality is an important aspect of this composition, it is not used with complete consistency. (This is the one feature that distinguishes this composition from the mature style.) None the less, even though IH-combinatoriality is not always explicitly present, it still exerts a powerful control over the harmonic organization of this variation.

In the first few measures of the Introduction Schoenberg created a 0369 tetrachord that was not a segment of the set itself but, rather, the combination of the first two elements of two IH-combinatorially related set forms.

In Variation I Schoenberg elaborates on that idea. The set is stated in the lower winds and contrabass, preserving the contour, subdivisions, and phrasing of the Theme. At the same time an accompaniment is created from four other set forms (see Ex. 7.13). As can be seen in the example, in the first measures of the Variation the accompaniment consists of P-0 and P-3 stated in parallel motion. Answering this pair of set forms is I-0 and I-3, also in parallel motion. Both pairs of forms are isomorphically partitioned.

Although there are five set forms stated more or less simultaneously, the result is far from the opaque layering of Schoenberg's earlier serial works. Rather, the strict parallel motion and the choice of set forms continually reproduce the harmonic motto of the Introduction.

As can be seen in the example, the 0369 tetrachord virtually saturates the surface, appearing in every measure of the example. Of course, this tetrachord is not an explicit component of the set itself but, rather, a property of a set form when combined with its IH-combinatorial counterpart. Thus, in the first variation, even though IH-combinator-

I. Variation

Ex. 7.13 Variations for Orchestra, Op. 31 mm. 58–61: the beginning of the
first variation

iality does not control set form choice and is not used to produce aggregates, none the less, it retains an influence on significant features of the compositional surface.

The set forms of the accompaniment are limited to those eight forms (P-0, I-0, P-3, I-3, P-6, etc.) used in mm. 1–23 of the Introduction. This ensures that the 0369 tetrachord always appears with the pitch classes C♯ E G B♭, the pitch level of the original appearance of this tetrachord in the Introduction.

VARIATION II

In the discussion of the String Quartet No. 3 it was emphasized that isomorphic partitioning became a technique of central importance during this period. That observation can be supported by virtually every measure of the Variations A typical example is provided by the opening of Variation II (see Ex. 7.14). The accompaniment is created from two set forms, canonically related. The cello and bass clarinet present a partitioned statement of I-9 while the bassoon and flute answer with P-0.

These two set forms are isomorphically partitioned. For I-9, the cello is assigned order positions 0567te, the bass clarinet order positions 123489. For P-0, these same order-position assignments are given to the the bassoon and flute respectively.

This permits the formation of interesting invariant relationships. The pitch-class content of the cello line is equivalent to that of the flute line, that of the bass clarinet, equivalent to the bassoon.

The formation of such invariant relationships is hardly a surprise at this stage in Schoenberg's serial period. From virtually the beginning of his serial revolution Schoenberg experimented with the formation of invariants through isomorphic partitioning. What is significant about his handling of isomorphic partitioning in the Variations is the extraordinary variety of partitionings he found that produced interesting invariant relationships.

For instance, in Ex. 7.14, no sooner had Schoenberg finished with this first group of two set forms in the accompaniment (mm. 82–5) than he introduced a new pair: R-0 in the cello and cor anglais; RI-9 in the bass clarinet and bassoon. Here order positions 9850 from RI-9 and R-0 appear in the bassoon and cor anglais respectively. The pitch-class content is identical in both these parts: G-A♭-A-B♭, pitch-class set 0123, the tetrachord of the B-A-C-H motive. This partitioning is different from the hexachordal partitioning of mm. 82–5. An important aspect of this composition, and of all the mature compositions to come, is the exhaustiveness with which Schoenberg dissects the set, constantly looking for different partitionings that could be drawn from the set, and relating them by the isomorphic partitioning of other transformations.

Ex. 7.14 Variations for Orchestra, Op. 31, mm. 82–6: the beginning of the
second variation

VARIATION IV

One of Schoenberg's great accomplishments in this period was his refinement of multidimensional set presentations. The Variations for Orchestra demonstrate that the solution of the String Quartet No. 3 was no isolated act of compositional virtuosity, but a central feature of Schoenberg's mature handling of the twelve-tone system.

In this variation Schoenberg has created the middleground statement of the theme by extracting two elements from each local set form. Therefore, the beginning of the theme, P-o, unfolds over six local set statements (see Ex. 7.15). The specific choice of local set forms is determined by particular characteristics of the structure of the set. The set of the Variations for Orchestra is o 6 8 5 7 e 4 3 9 t 1 2. The interval classes of the six discrete dyads of this set are 6 3 4 1 1 1. If the set is divided into hexachords and the elements of equivalent hexachordal order position are compared, then the interval classes formed between elements of equivalent hexachordal order position are 4, 3, 1, 5, 6, 3 (see Ex. 7.16). That is, every interval class of the discrete dyads is also found between elements of identical hexachordal order position.

Schoenberg exploits this property to generate the middleground thematic statement of the set from the local set statements. In order to produce the first dyad of the theme, B♭-E, Schoenberg needed to partition his set so that order positions 4 and t are placed together in a line. For this to be at the proper transpositional level and in the right order Schoenberg had to choose one of the following set forms: R-e, P-5, RI-1, or I-7. Schoenberg chose P-5 and placed the extracted dyad, B♭-E, into a line played by the harp, celesta, and mandolin.

The next dyad is F♯-E♭. To produce this dyad Schoenberg had to partition his set so that either order positions 1 and 7, or 5 and e were conjoined. Schoenberg chose 1 and 7. Since the preceding set statement was a prime form, he had to use an inversional form to preserve the hierarchy of the slowly evolving principal melody. To place the notes in the correct order it was necessary to use a retrograde-inversion: RI-e.

In a similar manner Schoenberg generates the remaining elements of the principal melody. The result is a passage in which the set appears simultaneously in several dimensions, and in which the partitioning and the choice of local sets is determined by the structure of the set.

VARIATIONS V–IX

The multidimensional set presentation of the fifth variation was described in chapter 2. Nothing could better illustrate Schoenberg's versatility than the extraordinary range of different multidimensional presentations encountered in these four variations. It is important to re-

Ex. 7.15 Variations for Orchestra, Op. 31, mm. 130–9: the beginning of the
fourth variation with its multidimensional set presentation

cognize, as well, that each of these variations is unique: Schoenberg did
not simply use a stock formula but each time sought a different way to
draw from the set a multidimensional presentation.

In Variation VI the theme unfolds slowly, primarily in the first cello.
The notes of the theme are introduced a few at a time as elements of
local set forms. For instance, B♭-E-F♯-D♯, the first four notes of the

the set of Op. 31:   0 6 8 5 7 e 4 3 9 t 1 2
interval classes of the dyads: 6   3   4   1   1   1

interval classes between elements of like hexachordal order number:

(pitch-class numbers)

first hexachord: 0 6 8 5 7 e
second hexachord: 4 3 9 t 1 2
interval class between elements
of like hexachordal
order-position: 4 3 1 5 6 3

Ex. 7.16 Variations for Orchestra, Op. 31: interval classes of the disjunct
dyads and elements of like hexachordal order position

theme (P-0) are extracted from P-7 (order positions 35t9) in mm. 202–3. At the same time Schoenberg also partitioned other set forms to imitate or anticipate the segments of the gradually emerging theme. For example, in mm. 202–3, I-3 appears in the winds. The partitioning places order positions 1357te as a line in the flute and cor anglais. The first four notes of this line, G-A♭-B♭-D, form pitch-class set 0137, the same pitch-class set that is formed by the first four order positions of the set, and appears as the beginning of the theme in the solo cello.

In Variation VII Schoenberg experiments with retrograde isomorphic partitioning. The theme appears in the piccolo and glockenspiel (with doublings in the celesta and solo violin). Each local set form supplies one note of the slowly unfolding theme. Those local set forms occur in retrograde-isomorphically partitioned pairs. Thus, for example, in the first beat of m. 238 the solo violin has order positions 7 and 6 from RI-4 while in the next beat it has the retrograde-isomorphic segment order positions 4 and 5 from P-7. All the other segments in P-7 are similarly retrograde-isomorphically partitioned with respect to the equivalent segments in the preceding set form.

In Variation VIII Schoenberg experiments with yet another way to effect a multidimensional set presentation. The theme begins in m. 262 in the oboe with the first hexachord of I-9; the remaining elements of this set form appear in the strings in m. 263. And so it continues: each segment of the theme is complemented by the remaining elements of that set form in the accompaniment. A similar technique is used in Variation IX.

FINALE

The Finale, nearly as long as the rest of the work combined, is a *tour de force* of compositional and orchestrational brilliance. Here Schoenberg demonstrates his extraordinary freedom of invention, his assured handling of the twelve-tone method, his seemingly effortless exploitation of the properties of the set.

By this point in his career, all of the mature twelve-tone features have been developed. However, these features cannot be understood in isolation: the principal achievement of this period is the way in which all of the mature features appear not as separate elements but as components of an integrated musical system, touching upon every level of the musical fabric.

Two examples from the Finale should be sufficient to demonstrate the supreme mastery of Schoenberg's handling of the twelve-tone system at this stage of his career (see Ex. 7.17). From mm. 389–95 Schoenberg begins yet another multidimensional set presentation. However, this time he does not limit himself to the presentation of a single middleground set statement but, rather, presents two set forms: P-o in the oboe and I-6 in the horn.

These two middleground set presentations are formed by extracting elements from seven local set forms. From each of these forms Schoenberg draws several elements to form one or both of the two gradually unfolding lines. However, not even the juggling of these two lines is achieved at the expense of the harmonic structure: the succession of local set forms is chosen so that they proceed in pairs of IH-combinatorially related set forms, always ordered so that aggregates are created between the adjacent IH-combinatorially related set forms.

In another passage from the Finale, mm. 332–3, Schoenberg presents

Ex. 7.17 Variations for Orchestra, Op. 31, Finale, mm. 388–95

pairs of IH-combinatorially related set forms, stated contrapuntally, forming aggregates between order corresponding hexachords (see Ex. 7.18). The metre is thus created with aggregates marking off each beat, IH-combinatorially related pairs marking off each half-measure and each measure characterized by an IH-combinatorial complex. At the same time, each set form of m. 332 is isomorphically partitioned with respect to a set form in m. 333, with the resultant saturation of the surface with invariant pitch-class sets. Moreover, the B-A-C-H theme is partitioned out, pervading the passage with the 0123 tetrachord.

IH-combinatoriality, aggregate formation, isomorphic partitioning,

Ex. 7.18 Variations for orchestra, Op. 31, Finale: mm. 332–3

elegant invariants, pitch-derived metre, consistent harmonic relationships, multidimensional set presentations—these are the mature characteristics, and we see them in the Variations, not as separable elements, but as parts of an integrated whole.

Their presence in this composition is a mark of the extraordinary distance travelled by Schoenberg in his serial odyssey. We saw Schoenberg beginning with only the faintest hints of this mature style. With unmatched resolve he searched, criticized, and persevered, constantly experimenting with his method, continually learning new techniques. He learned to reconcile serial ordering and developing variation, discovered how to create invariants, sought to relate the form to the structure of the set, found ways to control the harmony, phrasing, and metre. He did not accomplish this overnight, but only after a long and arduous compositional journey. Consider these passages from the Variations well, for here, before our eyes, is Schoenberg's mature twelve-tone style.

Epilogue
Op. 32 and Beyond

WITH the completion of the Variations for Orchestra, Op.31, all of the features of the mature twelve-tone style were in place. Schoenberg's long and difficult compositional odyssey was over.

This is not to say that Schoenberg ceased to grow or to experiment—far from it. In the compositions that follow the Variations for Orchestra Schoenberg continued to find new ways of organizing his material and persisted in looking for more refined solutions to the problems of twelve-tone coherence.

Prominent among the features that distinguish his late twelve-tone technique from that of the works of the 1930s is his tendency to treat the (unordered) source hexachord as the fundamental building-block of musical structure. For example, in the Trio, Op.45, at least two sets are used, one with twelve elements, the other with eighteen. Since both of these sets use the same source hexachord, there are at least five different orderings of any given hexachord. Similarly, if less formally, in the Fantasy, Op.47, the piano accompaniment presents complementary, unordered hexachords to the ordered hexachords in the violin. (Of course, this tendency to treat the hexachord as a harmonic entity can be traced back to Op.27 No. 3 and the free doubling of the vocal lines.)

There are other experiments as well. In the second movement of the Fourth String Quartet, Schoenberg creates a new ordering for the hexachord by partitioning out order positions 012678 of the original set. In the *Ode to Napoleon* Schoenberg tried to reconcile twelve-tone serialism and triadic tonality. The source hexachord (pitch-class set 014589) is ordered so that triads result from several different partitionings of each hexachord. Moreover, in *Der erste Psalm*, Op.50c, Schoenberg employed a *Wunderreihe* with its retrograde equal to a transposition of the set.

None the less, even though a degree of experimentation would always characterize Schoenberg's compositional approach, the techniques developed in the period 1914–28 would remain the basis of Schoenberg's twelve-tone method through all of the compositions after Op.31. This is so because these were not isolated features, but an integrated compositional idea, one in which phrasing, form, rhythm, metre, developing variation, and harmony were related to one another by the structure of the referential set. This was a true musical revolution, a complete rethinking of the nature of musical coherence. Schoenberg's thorough understanding of the possibilities of the twelve-tone system is an enduring testament to the artistic courage and compositional brilliance of one of the most profound musical thinkers of all time. We are witness to a composer who, with no model to work from and no guide to direct him, taught himself how to become a twelve-tone composer. With unmatched perseverence he continued learning until he had discovered how to relate all dimensions of the musical fabric to the referential set.

It should not be concluded, however, that Schoenberg's onward stylistic progress invalidated his earlier compositions, or that the early twelve-tone compositions are, necessarily, artistically inferior. The composer of *Moses und Aron* was also the composer of *Gurrelieder*, the *Kammersymphonie* No. 1 and *Pierrot*.

Typically, Schoenberg said it best:

There is no falling into order, because there was never disorder. There is no falling at all, but on the contrary, there is an ascending to higher and better order.[1]

---

[1] From a letter to Nicolas Slonimsky in which Schoenberg described the origins of his twelve-tone method. Slonimsky, *Music Since 1900* (4th edn., New York, 1971), 1316.

Glossary

The following informal definitions are designed to help the reader who has had little experience with twelve-tone theory. For more formal and extensive discussions of the terms and concepts described here consult the works listed in the bibliography, particularly those of Babbitt, Perle, and Forte.

AGGREGATE. A collection of twelve different pitches with each pitch class represented once and only once—other than immediate repetitions of notes and groups of notes—within the collection. (By this use of the term the twelve-tone set and the secondary set can be regarded as specific kinds of aggregates.) The aggregate must be distinguished from the weighted aggregate and from chromatic completion. The weighted aggregate is a collection of twelve pitches in which the twelfth pitch does not appear until after, at least, one pitch class has been represented at least twice, with each of these representations supplied by segments of different set forms. Chromatic completion refers to the less rigorous procedure of introducing all twelve pitch classes in a given passage without regard for duplication and where the repeated pitch classes are not necessarily elements of different set forms.

CHROMATIC COMPLETION. See under aggregate.

DIFFERENCE VECTOR. See under interval vector.

HEXACHORDAL INVERSIONAL COMBINATORIALITY. The property of certain hexachords such that under inversion at a given odd transposition none of the pitch classes of the original hexachord is preserved. Therefore, the transposed inversion together with the original level of the hexachord forms an aggregate. For example, the combination of D C♯ A B♭ F E♭, the first hexachord of P-o of Schoenberg's Op. 37, together with the first hexachord of I-5, G A♭ C B E F♯, includes all twelve pitch classes.

INDEX NUMBER. Denotes the fixed numerical value of the sum of the pitch-class numbers of notes of the same order position in inversionally related set forms. For example, the first pitch (D) of Schoenberg's Op. 37 may be assigned the number o. Therefore, the first element of I-5 (G) is 5. The sum of these two pitch-class numbers, from identical order positions in their respective set forms, is 5, the index number. Any other pair of notes of like order position from this same pair of set forms will yield this index number. For instance, the second element of P-o is e (eleven), the second element of I-5, 6. $6 + e$ (modulo 12) $= 5$; the third element of P-o is 7, the third of I-5 is t (ten); $7 + t = 5$ (modulo 12).

INTERVAL CLASS. Denotes both an interval and its complement. Intervals larger than 6 are described by their complements (e $= 1$, t $= 2$, $9 = 3$, $8 = 4$, $7 = 5$). Thus 3 semitones and 9 semitones are both considered members of the same interval class, interval class 3.

INTERVAL VECTOR. The interval-class content of a pitch-class set represented as an ordered array of integers. An interval vector is notated by a string of numbers, separated by commas, enclosed within braces. Each numeral in the string indicates how many instances of a given interval class are present within the collection. The first entry indicates the number of occurrences of interval class 1, the second entry the number of occurrences of interval class 2, etc. For example pitch-class set 024579 has the interval vector {1,4,3,2,5,0}. This indicates that there is one instance of interval class 1, four of interval class 2, three of interval class 3, two of interval class 4, five of interval class 5, and none of interval class 6. Similarly, the difference vector details the intervals formed between two discrete collections. It is notated in the same manner as the interval vector.

INVARIANTS. Relationships of a set preserved under a given operation. Some invariants are fixed properties of the twelve-tone system (for example, interval order is always held fixed under transposition). Other invariant relationships are dependent on the specific ordering or content of a segment of the set and the particular transformation chosen. For example, in the set C♯ F E♭ G A B♭ B D C E G♯ F♯, the first trichord contains the pitch classes C♯ F E♭. At I-4 the first three elements are F C♯ E♭. That is, the first trichord of P-0 is invariant at I-4.

ISOMORPHIC PARTITIONING. Denotes the partitioning of two set forms according to an identical order-number scheme. For example, if P-0 of Op. 37 is partitioned into two instruments such that order positions 02468t (D A F E A♭ F♯) are assigned to one voice and 13579e (C♯ B♭ E♭ C G B) to the other, and if I-5 is similarly partitioned (G C E, etc., A♭ B F♯, etc.), then the sets are said to be isomorphically partitioned.

ORDER NUMBER. Describes the relative temporal position of an element of a set. The first element of the set is assigned order position '0', the second element '1', and so forth.

PITCH CLASS. Denotes a class of pitches related by octave equivalence. Thus, for instance, any D, regardless of registral placement, is a member of pitch class D. Enharmonic spellings have no significance in the twelve-tone system. Thus, for example, E♭ and D♯ are members of the same pitch class.

PITCH-CLASS SET. A set of distinct integers, representing pitch classes. Pitch-class sets are notated by a string of integers without spaces between the entries. Thus, C♯ D F G is pitch-class set 0146. Pitch-class sets are named according to their normal order. This is determined by placing the elements of a collection (eliminating duplications) within an octave in ascending order, so arranged that there is the smallest possible interval between the lowest and highest elements of the collection (e.g., G♯ A C E, not C E G♯ A). If there is more than one such compact ordering, the ordering is chosen that yields the smallest interval between the lowest (or the highest, see below) element and the next element in the collection (e.g., G♯ A C E, not E G♯ A C). Once this ordering has been established, then the lowest (or the highest, see below) element is assigned the value 0 and the distance from that element to the remaining elements is measured up in semitones (for example, for the collection G♯ A C E,

G♯ is assigned 0, then G♯ to A = 1, G♯ to C = 4, G♯ to E = 8; therefore, G♯ A C E = pitch-class set 0148). If the interval from the highest note to the preceding note in the collection is smaller than the interval from the lowest element to the next element, the value 0 is assigned instead to the highest element and the distance to the remaining elements is measured in semitones descending from the origin (for example, C E F = pitch-class set 015, *not* 045). Two unordered collections are said to be equivalent if they can be reduced to the same normal order. Thus, the collections C♯ D F G and A G♯ F E♭ are equivalent: both are pitch-class set 0146.

TWELVE-TONE SET. Denotes a referential ordering of the twelve pitch classes. 'Twelve-tone set' or 'basic set' are Schoenberg's preferred terms in English. (Others refer to this as 'twelve-tone row', 'twelve-note row', or 'series'.) Twelve-tone sets may be subjected to the operations of transposition, inversion, and retrograde, either individually or in combination. All forty-eight transformations—twelve transpositions of the prime, inversional, retrograde, and retrograde inversional versions—derivable from a given referential ordering are considered to be *forms* of the same set. Twelve-tone sets may be represented in numerical form (pitch-class numbers). The first pitch class of the set—the origin—is assigned the number '0' and the subsequent elements of the set are calculated by counting in semitones from the origin. The first statement of the set of Schoenberg's Fourth String Quartet, Op. 37, appears as D C♯ A B♭ F E♭ E C A♭ G F♯ B. In numerical form, therefore, this would be 0 11 7 8 3 1 2 10 6 5 4 9. In this book the convention has been adopted of representing the integers '10' and '11' with the mnemonic symbols 't' and 'e'. This is done to avoid possible confusion in strings of numbers, for example, does 10 mean 1,0 or 10? Twelve-tone operations are best defined arithmetically. Transposition should be thought of as the addition (modulo 12) of a constant to each element of a given set. For example (P-0) 0 e 7 8 3 1 2 t 6 5 4 9 at a transposition of 6 becomes 6 5 1 2 9 7 8 4 0 e t 3, that is, 6 is added to each element of P-0 (0 + 6 = 6, e + 6 = 5, 7 + 6 = 1, etc.) Inversion is defined as complementation to 12 of each element of the set, i.e. 12 − a = b, where 'a' is an element of a set and 'b' is the corresponding element in I. For example, I-0 of the set above is formed as follows: 12 − 0 = 0, 12 − 11 (e) = 1, 12 − 7 = 5, 12 − 8 = 4, etc. Thus I-0 is 0 1 5 4 9 e t 2 6 7 8 3. Retrograde can be defined as the complementation to 11 of order numbers. Thus the first element of P-0, order position 0, becomes the twelfth element of R-0, order position e (11). In this book, however, as explained in the text, the convention has been adopted of representing the order numbers of retrograde forms in descending order: e t 9 8 7 . . . 2 1 0. The transformations of sets are labelled as follows. Prime forms (the form of the set in its first compositional representation) have the label 'P', inversions 'I', retrogrades 'R', and retrograde inversions 'RI'. For P- and I-forms transpositions are indicated by a numerical suffix denoting the transpositional constant. Retrogrades and retrograde-inversions, however, are identified according to the transpositional level of the P- and I-forms of which they are retrogrades. Thus, the retrograde of 0 e 7 8 3 1 2 t 6 5 4 9 is assigned the label R-0, *not* R-9.

Bibliography

Babbitt, Milton, 'Some Aspects of Twelve-Tone Composition', *Score*, 12 (1955), 53–61.

—— 'Twelve-Tone Invariants as Compositional Determinants', *Musical Quarterly*, 46 (1960), 246–59. Reprinted in Paul Henry Lang (ed.), *Problems of Modern Music* (New York, 1962), 108–21.

—— 'Set Structure as a Compositional Determinant', *Journal of Music Theory*, 5 (1961), 72–94. Reprinted in Benjamin Boretz and Edward Cone (edd.), *Perspectives on Contemporary Music Theory* (New York, 1972), 129–47.

—— 'Twelve-Tone Rhythmic Structure and the Electronic Medium', *Perspectives of New Music*, 1 (1962), 49–79. Reprinted in Benjamin Boretz and Edward Cone (edd.), *Perspectives on Contemporary Music Theory* (New York, 1972), 148–79

—— 'Mr Babbitt Answers', *Perspectives of New Music* 2 (1963), 128–32.

—— 'The Structure and Function of Musical Theory'. *College Music Symposium*, 5 (1965), 49–60. Reprinted in Benjamin Boretz and Edward Cone (edd.), *Perspectives on Contemporary Music Theory* (*New York, 1972*), 10–21.

—— 'Three Essays on Schoenberg', in Benjamin Boretz and Edward Cone (edd.), (rev. edn., New York, 1972), 47–60.

—— 'Since Schoenberg', *Perspectives of New Music*, 12 (1973–4), 3–28.

Bailey, Walter, *Programmatic Elements in the Works of Arnold Schoenberg* (Ann Arbor, 1984).

Beach, David, 'Segmental Invariance and the Twelve-Tone System', *Journal of Music Theory*, 20 (1976), 157–84.

Boulez, Pierre, 'Schoenberg is Dead', *Score*, 6 (1952), 18–22.

Christensen, Jean, 'Schoenberg's Sketches for *Die Jakobsleiter*: A Study of a Special Case', *Journal of the Arnold Schoenberg Institute*, 2 (1978), 112–21.

Dahlhaus, Carl, *Arnold Schönberg Variationen für Orchester, op. 31* (Munich: 1968).

Forte, Alan, *The Structure of Atonal Music* (New Haven and London, 1973).

Frisch, Walter, *Brahms and the Principle of Developing Variation* (Berkeley, 1984).

Graziano, John, 'Serial Procedures in Schoenberg's Op. 23', *Current Musicology*, 13 (1972), 58–63.

Haimo, Ethan, 'Editing Schoenberg's Twelve-Tone Music', *Journal of the Arnold Schoenberg Institute*, 8 (1984), 141–57.

—— 'Redating Schoenberg's Passacaglia for Orchestra', *Journal of the American Musicological Society*, 40 (1987), 471–94.

—— and Paul Johnson, 'Isomorphic Partitioning and Schoenberg's Fourth String Quartet', *Journal of Music Theory*, 28 (1984), 47–72.

Hamao, Fusako, 'On the Origin of the Twelve-Tone Method: Schoenberg's Sketches for the Unfinished *Symphony* (1914–1915)', *Current Musicology* 42 (1986), 32–45.

Hindemith, Paul, *The Craft of Musical Composition*, Book I, trans. Arthur Mendel (4th edn., New York, 1945).

Hyde, Martha, 'The Telltale Sketches: Harmonic Structure in Schoenberg's Twelve-Tone Method', *Musical Quarterly*, 66 (1980), 560–80.

—— 'The Roots of Form in Schoenberg's Sketches', *Journal of Music Theory*, 24 (1980), 1–36.

—— *Schoenberg's Twelve-Tone Harmony* (Ann Arbor, 1982).

—— 'The Format and Function of Schoenberg's Twelve-Tone Sketches', *Journal of the American Musicological Society*, 36 (1983), 453–80.

—— 'A Theory of Twelve-Tone Meter', *Music Theory Spectrum*, 6 (1984), 14–51.

—— 'Musical Form and The Development of Schoenberg's Twelve-Tone Method', *Journal of Music Theory*, 29 (1985), 85–143.

Journal of the Arnold Schoenberg Institute, ed. Leonard Stein (1976–).

Klemm, Eberhardt, 'Zur Theorie der Reihenstruktur und Reihendisposition in Schönbergs 4. Streichquartette', *Beiträge zur Musikwissenschaft*, 8 (1966), 27–49.

Lake, William, 'Structural Functions of Segmental Interval-Class 1 Dyads in Schoenberg's Fourth Quartet, First Movement', *In Theory Only*, 8 (1984), 21–9.

Lester, Joel, 'Pitch Structure Articulation in the Variations of Schoenberg's Serenade', *Perspectives of New Music*, 6 (1968), 22–34.

Lewin, David, 'A Theory of Segmental Association', *Perspectives of New Music*, 1 (1962), 89–116. Reprinted in Benjamin Boretz and Edward Cone (edd.), *Perspectives on Contemporary Music Theory* (New York, 1972), 180–207.

—— 'A Study of Hexachord Levels in Schoenberg's Violin Fantasy', *Perspectives of New Music*, 6 (1968), 18–32. Reprinted in Benjamin Boretz and Edward Cone (edd.), *Perspectives on Schoenberg and Stravinsky* (rev. edn. New York, 1972), 78–92.

Maegaard, Jan, 'A Study in the Chronology of op. 23–26 by Arnold Schoenberg', *Dansk aarbog for musikforskning*, 2 (1962), 93–115.

—— *Studien zur Entwicklung des dodekaphonen Satzes bei Arnold Schönberg*, 2 vol. and suppl. (Notenbeilage) (Copenhagen, 1972).

—— 'Schönbergs Zwölftonreihen', *Die Musikforschung*, 29 (1976), 385–425.

—— 'Om den kronologiske placering af Schönbergs klaverstykke op. 23 nr. 3', *Musik en forskning*, 2 (1976), 5–10.

Martino, Donald, 'The Source Set and Its Aggregate Formations', *Journal of Music Theory*, 5 (1961), 224–73.

Mead, Andrew, 'Pedagogically Speaking: Manifestations of Pitch-Class Order', *In Theory Only*, 8 (1984), 23–32.

—— 'Large-Scale Strategy in Schoenberg's Twelve-Tone Music', *Perspectives of New Music*, 24 (1985), 120–57.

—— '"Tonal" Forms in Arnold Schoenberg's Twelve-Tone Music', *Music Theory Spectrum*, 9 (1987), 67–92.

Möllers, Christian, *Reihentechnik und musikalische Gestalt bei Arnold Schönberg: eine Untersuchung zum III. Streichquartett op 30*, Beihefte zum Archiv für Musikwissenschaft, xvii (Wiesbaden, 1977).

Oesch, Hans, 'Schönberg im Vorfeld der Dodekaphonie', *Melos*, 41 (1974), 330–8.

Peles, Steven, 'Interpretations of Sets in Multiple Dimensions: Notes on the Second Movement of Arnold Schoenberg's *String Quartet # 3*', *Perspectives of New Music*, 22 (1983–4), 303–52.

Perle, George, 'Babbitt, Lewin, and Schoenberg: A Critique', *Perspectives of New Music*, 2 (1963), 120–7.

—— *Serial Composition and Atonality* (5th edn., Los Angeles, 1981), 96–101.

Rahn, John, 'On Pitch or Rhythm: Interpretations of Ordering of and in Pitch and Time', *Perspectives of New Music*, 13 (1975), 182–203.

Rufer, Josef, *Composition with Twelve Tones*, trans. Humphrey Searle (New York, 1954).

—— *The Works of Arnold Schoenberg*, trans. Dika Newlin (London, 1962).

Schoenberg, Arnold, *Briefe*, ed. Erwin Stein (Mainz, 1958).

—— *Sämtliche Werke*, ed. Josef Rufer *et al.* (Vienna, 1966–).

—— 'Vortrag/12 TK/Princeton', ed. Claudio Spies, *Perspectives of New Music*, 13 (1974), 58–136.

—— *Style and Idea*, ed. Leonard Stein, trans. Leo Black (New York, 1975).

Slonimsky, Nicolas, *Music Since 1900* (4th edn., New York, 1971).

Smith, Joan, *Schoenberg and His Circle: A Viennese Portrait* (New York, 1986).

Starr, Daniel, 'Derivation and Polyphony', *Perspectives of New Music*, 23 (1984), 180–257.

—— and Robert Morris, 'A General Theory of Combinatoriality and the Aggregate', *Perspectives of New Music*, 16 (1977), 3–35 (Part 1) and *Perspectives of New Music*, 16 (1978), 50–84 (Part 2).

Stuckenschmidt, Hans Heinz, *Schoenberg: His Life, World and Work*, trans. Humphrey Searle (New York, 1977).

Webern, Anton, *The Path to the New Music* trans. Leo Black (Bryn Mawr, 1963).

Westergaard, Peter, 'Toward a Twelve-Tone Polyphony', *Perspectives of New Music*, 4 (1966), 90–112. Reprinted in Benjamin Boretz and Edward Cone (edd.), *Perspectives on Contemporary Music Theory* (New York, 1972) 238–60.

Whittal, Arnold, *Schoenberg Chamber Music* (Seattle, 1972).

Wille Rudolf, 'Reihentechnik in Schönbergs op. 19, 2', *Die Musikforschung*, 19 (1966), 42–3.

Zillig, Winfried, 'Notes on Arnold Schoenberg's Unfinished Oratorio "Die Jakobsleiter"', *Score*, 25 (1959), 7–16.

Index